The American Revolution: Step-by-Step Activities to Engage Children in Why the American Colonists Went to War Against Great Britain, including the Struggles of the Colonists, a Reader's Theater, Timelines, and More!

Acknowledgements

The American Revolution: Step-by-Step Activities to Engage Children in Why the American Colonists Went to War Against Great Britain, including the Struggles of the Colonists, a Reader's Theater, Timelines, and More!

AUTHOR

Priscilla H. Porter is the Director of the Porter History-Social Science Resource Center located at the Palm Desert Campus of California State University San Bernardino. A former elementary teacher, Dr. Porter is the author of numerous curriculum guides and is the senior author of *Reflections*, a Kindergarten to Grade 6 social studies textbook series published by Harcourt School Publishers

Contributors to this curriculum guide include:

Kimberly Clarke, Desert Sands Unified School District
Dr. Rhoda Coleman, University of Southern California
Rhonda Fort, Palm Springs Unified School District
Kirsten Hill, Desert Sands Unified School District
Diana Parsons, Los Nietos School District
Karen Sanders, King's Schools, Palm Springs
David Vigilante, San Diego Unified School District, Retired
Stacey Ward, Palm Springs Unified School District

Notes from the Author

The first book in the Step-By-Step series for teachers of American History is *Settling the Colonies.* It is available on www.amazon.com. To hear about my latest books, sign up for my exclusive **New Release Mailing List** by sending me an email at prisporter@aol.com

Requesting Your Review

Reviews are especially important to authors. If you have enjoyed this book, please write a review of it on www.amazon.com

Direct inquiries to: Dr. Priscilla Porter
Palm Desert Campus, California State University San Bernardino
37-500 Cook Street
Palm Desert, California 92211

The American Revolution

Description of the Unit

The focus of this unit is on the major events that led to the American Revolution, including the struggles the citizens endured to gain their freedom. The many complexities of the American Revolution cannot be covered in these short lessons. This unit serves as an introduction to the topic and provides a baseline for further study.

Lesson 1 begins by creating a timeline of events that serves as a scaffold on which they can hang the names and events related to the American Revolution. Drawing on information from multiple print or digital sources, students quickly locate dates for a list of events and quote accurately from the source when defending their answer. While creating this *Timeline of the American Revolution*, students are exposed to academic, domain-specific vocabulary and the names and brief descriptions of key events.

Lesson 2 is a simulation in which the "Royal Tax Commissioners" stamp all papers written by students and force them to pay a "tax" or imprisonment. **Lesson 3** is a two-day activity during which students perform five Readers' Theater plays, and they create protest posters that reveal what the colonists felt were unfair and ultimately brought about the revolution.

Lesson 4 shows the use of artwork as propaganda (Paul Revere's Boston Massacre). Students analyze the engraving from an artistic perspective and by putting themselves "in the picture." The Boston Tea Party and the Coercive (Intolerable) Acts are the focus of **Lesson 5**. In **Lesson 6**, a narrative text (*Katie's Trunk*) is used to enrich the study of history by using literature about the period. The story reveals the way people saw themselves, their ideas, and their fears. Multiple viewpoints are introduced along with a decision-making activity in which students evaluate the decisions of the main character.

Lesson 7 looks at the role of Colonial Women during the American Revolution. In **Lesson 8**, students work to understand the people and events associated with the drafting and signing of the Declaration of Independence. They determine the meaning of domain-specific words, read, and comprehend informational text, and explain the relationships or interactions between two or more events.

In **Lesson 9**, excerpts from Thomas Paine's *The American Crisis* are analyzed along with the conditions at Valley Forge during the brutal winter of 1777-78. **Lesson 10** analyzes the shortcomings of the Articles of Confederation. The war finally ends in **Lesson 11** with The Treaty of Paris. **Lesson 12** returns to the *Timeline of the American Revolution* to place key events of the revolution in chronological order and use multiple print and digital sources to identify events, key people, and the causes and effects of the American Revolution.

Compelling Question: Why did the American Colonists go to war against Great Britain?

Supporting Questions:

Lesson 1: A Timeline of the American Revolution
How do I use multiple print and digital sources to locate specific information?
What were the major events of the American Revolution and in what order did they occur?

Lesson 2: The Stamp Act and the Townshend Acts
Why did the colonists begin to rebel against Great Britain?

Lesson 3: What was Unfair?
What disagreements led to the American Revolution?

Lesson 4: The Boston Massacre
What were the multiple causes and effects of the Boston Massacre?

Lesson 5: The Boston Tea Party and the Coercive Acts
Why did the Sons of Liberty dump crates of British tea into Boston Harbor?
What was the British response to the Boston Tea Party?
How effective was the Boston Tea Party?

Lesson 6: Katie's Trunk
What happened to a family who remained loyal to England?

Lesson 7: The Role of Colonial Women During the American Revolution
What different roles did women play during the American Revolution?
What were the trade-offs and opportunity costs in the decision to boycott British goods?

Lesson 8: The Declaration of Independence
What is the Declaration of Independence and how did it mark the creation of a new nation?

Lesson 9: Thomas Paine's *The American Crisis* and The Brutal Winter at Valley Forge
What was the impact of Thomas Paine's *The American Crisis*?
What were the conditions at Valley Forge during the brutal winter of 1777-78?

Lesson 10: The Articles of Confederation
What was the purpose of the Articles of Confederation?
What were the weaknesses of the Articles of Confederation?

Lesson 11: The Treaty (Peace) of Paris
How did the British army compare with the Continental army?
What were the reasons for the victory over the British at Yorktown?

Lesson 12: Freedom's Journey
What were the key events of the American Revolution?

History-Social Science Content Standards
Students explain the Causes of the American Revolution
Understand how political, religious, and economic ideas and interests brought about the Revolution (e.g. resistance to imperial policy, the Stamp Act, the Townsend Acts, taxes on tea, Coercive Acts).
Understand the people and events associated with the drafting and signing of the Declaration of Independence and the document's significance, including the key political concepts it embodies, the origins of those concepts, and its role in severing ties with Great Britain.

Historical and Social Sciences Analysis Skills
Chronological and Spatial Thinking
Students place key events and people of the historical era they are studying in a chronological sequence and within a spatial context; they interpret timelines.

Research, Evidence, and Point of View
Students pose relevant questions about events they encounter in historical documents, eyewitness accounts, maps, and artworks.

Historical Interpretation
Students summarize the key events of the era they are studying and explain the historical contents of those events.
Students identify and interpret the multiple causes and effects of historical events.

Common Core State Standards for English Language Arts

Activities are included in this unit to develop standards for reading, writing, listening, and speaking. Refer to the abbreviations listed throughout the unit. For example, RI 5.1 refers to Reading for Informational Text, Grade 5, Standard 1

Reading Standards for Information Text (RI)

RI 5.1 Quote accurately from a text when explaining what the text says explicitly.

RI 5.2 Determine two or more main ideas of a text and explain how they are supported by key details; summarize the text.

RI 5.4 Determine the meaning of general academic and domain-specific words or phrases in a text relevant to a grade 5 topic or subject area.

RI 5.5 Compare and contrast the overall structure (e.g., chronology, cause/effect) of events in two or more texts.

RI 5.6 Draw upon information from multiple print or digital sources, demonstrating the ability to locate an answer to a question quickly.

RI 5.8 Explain how an author uses reasons and evidence to support particular points in a text, identifying which reasons and evidence support which point(s).

Reading Standards for Literature

RL 5.2 Determine the theme of a story, drama, or poem from details in the text, including how characters in a story respond to challenges.

RL 5.3 Compare and contrast two or more characters, drawing upon specific details in the text (e.g, how characters interact).

Writing Standards (W)

W. 5.1 Write opinion pieces on topics or texts, supporting a point of view with reasons and information.

W 5.3 Write narratives to develop real or imagined experiences or events using effective technique, descriptive details, and clear event sequences.

W 5.7 Conduct short research projects that use several sources to build knowledge through investigation of different aspects of a topic.

W 5.8 Gather relevant information from print or digital sources; summarize or paraphrase information and provide a list of sources.

Speaking and Listening Standards (SL)

SL 5.1 Engage effectively in a range of collaborative discussions (one-on-one), in groups, and teacher-led) with diverse partners on grade 5 topics and texts, building on each other's ideas and expressing their own clearly.

SL 5.2 Summarize a written text read aloud or information presented in diverse media and formats, including visually, quantitatively, and orally.

SL 5.3 Summarize the points a speaker or media source makes and explain how each claim is supported by reasons and evidence.

Lesson 1: A Timeline of the American Revolution

Supporting Questions
- How do I use multiple print and digital sources to locate specific information?
- What were the major events of the American Revolution and in what order did they occur?

Preparation: Create a large class timeline on a bulletin board. Begin at 1760 and end at 1790. Mark every ten years with a long vertical line and the rest of the years with short vertical lines.

Materials needed: a copy of the **Timeline Event Cards** (Handout #1.1, page 9) cut into strips; for each pair of students, a copy of multiple print sources (textbooks, non-fiction books), and access to digital sources.

Activity #1 Scavenger Hunt

Note: In this activity, students are exposed to academic, domain-specific vocabulary and the names and brief descriptions of key events (RI 5.4). The timeline serves as a scaffold for the vocabulary, people, dates, and events of the American Revolution.

Step 1: Timeline Event Cards Tell students they will be given a card with information related to the Revolutionary War. Working with a partner, they will go on a scavenger hunt to quickly locate the date of the event (RI 5.6), note the location of the source for their answer, and then put the event in chronological order on a timeline. Explain that there are multiple print and digital sources available with the information they need.

Show the first timeline event card, "The Stamp Act is passed by Parliament." How can we find the date of this event? Demonstrate how to use the index of an available history book by working together as a group to locate the date for this event.

Explain that an **index** is an alphabetized list of subjects that gives the page or pages on which each item is mentioned. It is a reference tool to help you find a specific topic more quickly. To use an index, you need to know the **key words** for the subject. Ask students what key words should be used to find the information they need for this event. (Stamp Act)

Have all students **skim**, or read quickly, down the page to look for the date this event took place. Be careful, other dates may be listed, For example, 1764 is the date Parliament passed the Sugar Act, not the Stamp Act. Once students identify 1765 as the correct date, write it on the timeline strip. On the back of the strip, write the source and page number (or website address) where the correct date was located. This will be useful later when students are asked to verify the source where they found the correct date.

Do the next two events together with the class. "The **Townshend Acts** are passed by Parliament." "The **Boston Massacre** takes place." (An Answer Key with the correct dates is located on the next page.)

Step 2: Pairs Scavenger Hunt Distribute one or two of the timeline event strips (Handout #1.1) to each pair of students. After the students investigate to find the date, they write it on the paper strip and, on the back of the strip, write the source and page numbers (or website address) where the correct date was found (RI 5.6). Continue until all dates have been located.

Step 3: Verify Accuracy After all the dates have been found, have each pair read their event card/s, give the correct date, and provide the source where the date was found.

As each event is read, have all students turn to the source to "verify" the date for accuracy (RI 5.1).

Once the date has been verified, post the event strip in the correct location on the class timeline.

Activity #2 Individual Timelines (Optional)

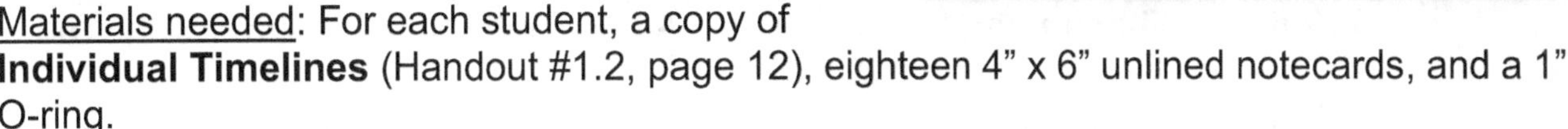
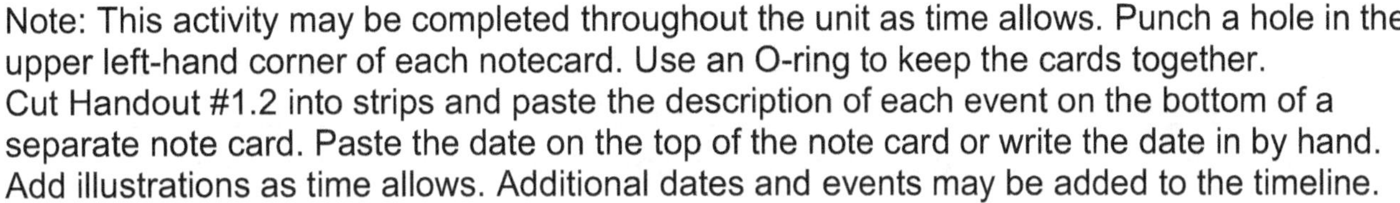

Materials needed: For each student, a copy of **Individual Timelines** (Handout #1.2, page 12), eighteen 4" x 6" unlined notecards, and a 1" O-ring.

Note: This activity may be completed throughout the unit as time allows. Punch a hole in the upper left-hand corner of each notecard. Use an O-ring to keep the cards together. Cut Handout #1.2 into strips and paste the description of each event on the bottom of a separate note card. Paste the date on the top of the note card or write the date in by hand. Add illustrations as time allows. Additional dates and events may be added to the timeline.

Assessment
➢ Quickly locate dates and verify the source to show skill in using multiple print sources.
➢ Create individual timeline cards with the date, the event, and an illustration (optional)

Answer Key: Words listed in BOLD are the Key Words.

1765	The **Stamp Act** is passed by Parliament. It places a tax on paper documents in the colonies, such as newspapers, documents, and playing cards.
1767	The **Townshend Acts** are passed by Parliament. They tax imports such as glass, tea, paint, and paper brought into the colonies.
1770	The **Boston Massacre** takes place.
1773	The **Tea Act** is passed by Parliament.
1773	The **Boston Tea Party** takes place to protest the Tea Act. The Sons of Liberty dress as Mohawk Indians, board the British ships, and throw crates of tea into Boston Harbor.
1774	The **Coercive Acts** are passed by Parliament. It forces the people to obey the laws. Colonists say the new laws are "Intolerable."
1774	The **First Continental Congress** opens in Philadelphia.
1775	The **Battles** of **Lexington** and **Concord** are fought. Colonists form militia units called **Minutemen.** They are called Minutemen because they were said to be ready to fight at a minute's notice.

1775	The **Second Continental Congress** meets in Philadelphia.
1776	Thomas Paine publishes ***Common Sense***. This pamphlet (short book) argues that the colonies should claim their independence.
1776	The **Declaration of Independence** was signed by Congress. On July 2, 1776, Congress voted to accept the Declaration's final wording, but it was not signed until two days later July 4, 1776.
1777	The **Articles of Confederation** are signed by Congress. It is the country's first government.
1777	General George Washington sets up winter quarters at **Valley Forge**.
1778	**Friedrich Wilheim von Steuben** trains American troops at Valley Forge. The soldiers become an organized army.
1780	**General Benedict Arnold** agrees to turn over the fort at West Point in return for money and a command in the British army. He is labeled a **traitor**.
1781	The French military and naval forces join with Washington to defeat the British. The British surrender to the Americans at **Yorktown**.
1781	The **Articles of Confederation** are **approved** (ratified) by the states.
1783	The **Treaty of Paris** ends the American Revolution. It officially names the United States of America as a new country.

Extended Activities: Famous People to Research

As time allows, assign, or have students select a name to research. Timeline cards may be made and added to the American Revolution Timeline.

- Abigail Adams
- John Adams
- Charles Cornwallis
- John Dickenson
- Benjamin Franklin
- Nathan Hale
- Patrick Henry
- King George the 3rd
- Thomas Jefferson
- Tadeusz Kosciuszko
- Marquis de Lafayette
- Gouverneur Morris
- Thomas Paine
- Molly Pitcher
- Paul Revere
- Baron Friedrich Wilhelm von Steuben
- Mercy Otis Warren
- George Washington
- Martha Washington
- Phyllis Wheatley

Additional Topics the students can research and add to the timeline

As time allows, assign or have students select other events to research. Timeline cards can be made and added to the *American Revolution Timeline*.

- Paul Revere's Ride
- The Proclamation of 1764
- The Quartering Act
- The Battle of Bunker Hill
- The Battle of Monmouth
- Battle of Saratoga

Timeline Event Cards

	The Stamp Act is passed by Parliament. It places a tax on paper documents in the colonies, such as newspapers, documents, and playing cards.
	The Townshend Acts are passed by Parliament. It taxes imports such as glass, tea, paint and paper brought into the colonies.
	The Boston Massacre takes place.
	The Tea Act is passed by Parliament.
	The Boston Tea Party takes place to protest the Tea Act. The Sons of Liberty dress as Mohawk Indians, board the British ships, and throw crates of tea into Boston Harbor.

	The Coercive Acts are passed by Parliament. It forces people to obey the laws. Colonists say the new laws are "Intolerable."
	The First Continental Congress opens in Philadelphia.
	The Battles of Lexington and Concord are fought. Colonists form militia units called Minutemen. They must be ready to fight at a minute's notice.
	The Second Continental Congress meets in Philadelphia.
	Thomas Paine publishes *Common Sense.* This pamphlet (short book) argues that the colonies should claim their independence.
	The Declaration of Independence was signed by Congress.
	The Articles of Confederation are signed by Congress. It is the country's first government.

	General George Washington sets up winter quarters at Valley Forge.
	Friedrich Wilheim von Steuben trains American troops at Valley Forge. The soldiers become an organized army.
	General Benedict Arnold agrees to turn over the fort at West Point in return for money and a command in the British army. He is labeled a traitor.
	The French military and naval forces join with Washington to defeat the British. The British surrender to the Americans at Yorktown.
	The Articles of Confederation are approved (ratified) by the states.
	The Treaty of Paris ends the American Revolution. The treaty officially names the United States of America as a new country.

Individual Timelines

1765	The **Stamp Act** is passed by Parliament. It places a tax on paper documents in the colonies, such as newspapers, documents, and playing cards.
1767	The **Townshend Acts** are passed by Parliament. It taxes imports such as glass, tea, paint and paper brought into the colonies.
1770	The **Boston Massacre** takes place.
1773	The **Tea Act** is passed by Parliament.
1773	The **Boston Tea Party** takes place to protest the Tea Act. The Sons of Liberty dress as Mohawk Indians, board the British ships, and throw crates of tea into Boston Harbor
1774	The **Coercive Acts** are passed by Parliament. It forces the people to obey the laws. Colonists say the new laws are "Intolerable."
1774	The **First Continental Congress** opens in Philadelphia.
1775	The **Battles** of **Lexington** and **Concord** are fought. Colonists form militia units called **Minutemen.** They are called Minutemen because they were said to be ready to fight at a minute's notice.
1775	The **Second Continental Congress** meets in Philadelphia.
1776	Thomas Paine publishes ***Common Sense***. This pamphlet (short book) argues that the colonies should claim their independence.
1776	The **Declaration of Independence** was signed by Congress.
1777	The **Articles of Confederation** are signed by Congress. It is the country's first plan of government.
1777	General George Washington sets up winter quarters at **Valley Forge**.
1778	**Friedrich Wilheim von Steuben** trains American troops at Valley Forge. The soldiers become an organized army.
1780	**General Benedict Arnold** agrees to turn over the fort at West Point in return for money and a command in the British army. He is labeled a **traitor**.
1781	The French military and naval forces join with Washington to defeat the British. The British surrender to the Americans at **Yorktown**.
1781	The **Articles of Confederation** are **approved** (ratified) by the states.
1783	The **Treaty of Paris** ends the American Revolution. It officially names the United States of America as a new country.

Lesson 2: The Stamp Act and the Townshend Acts

Supporting Question: Why did the colonists begin to rebel against Great Britain?

Background Information: Explain to the students that England and France, with their respective Indian allies, had fought from 1754 to 1763 to decide who would rule North America. England won but was left with a huge war debt. To help pay the cost of the war, Parliament placed taxes on many goods coming into the colonies.

The Stamp Act required the colonists to paste a stamp on all printed material issued in America. This included a stamp for each page of a newspaper, a will, contract, marriage license, diploma, playing cards, calendars and advertisements.

In 1767, Parliament passed the Townshend Acts. They levied taxes on British imports in America such as paper, glass, lead, paints, and tea. The Americans resisted and ordered a boycott of British goods. What angered the colonists is that they had no part in the making of the tax laws. The colonists felt they should not be taxed by a Parliament that did not represent them. A familiar cry was, "No taxation without representation."

Not everyone agreed. Some colonists, known as Loyalists or Tories felt the colonies should be more grateful to the Parliament and the King. They perceived themselves as fully British. Resistance against British rule grew. Eventually, the British Parliament gave in and in 1770 they cancelled all the Townshend taxes except for one – a three-penny-per-pound tax on tea.

Activity # 1 Taxation without Representation

Materials needed: For the teacher, a crown for King George (made with yellow construction paper); For 2-3 tax commissioners, arm bands, stamps, and an ink pad.

Instructions for the Teacher: The following activity is designed to help students understand how the colonists felt when they were forced to pay taxes without any representation to the British Parliament. The simulation should be an integral part of your "classroom day," not a separate event, in the same way that taxation became a part of everyday colonial life. You will need several "stamps," not postage stamps, but self-stamping stamps or stamps with a stamp pad. You may adapt any stamps that are on-hand regardless of what the statement is on the stamp. It is recommended that you conduct the activity during the morning so that any students who have to "pay taxes" may have their money or "collateral" returned before lunchtime.

Choose three or four students and take them outside the room. Tell them that you are King George III of England (it helps if you wear a gold crown). You are going to announce the new stamp tax. (See below for the announcement.)

The students are royal tax commissioners working in the American Colonies. Explain that it will be their job to announce the new "stamp tax," to affix "stamps" on all written documents, and to collect "taxes" from the colonists (students).

Instruct them that as they collect "taxes" from their classmates, they should keep the money in a safe place and keep a written record of the person, the tax, and the amount collected. They will be responsible to forward all taxes to King George at the end of the "year" (morning). Tie bands of cloth to the upper arms of the tax collectors and send them back inside to announce the new "stamp tax."

Step 1: Stamp It and Pay the Tax Upon returning to the classroom, the royal tax commissioners explain to the colonists that it is costing the school a lot of money to provide supplies for the students. Therefore a "tax" is going to be levied upon them for all papers they have written on. Have one of the tax commissioners read the "Stamp Tax announcement." (See box below.) Post a copy on the wall.

<table>
<tr><td align="center"><h2>Here Ye! Hear Ye!</h2></td></tr>
<tr><td align="center">By order of His Royal Highness, King George III, there will henceforth be a tax of one penny on all written documents in this room.</td></tr>
</table>

Have the royal tax commissioners ask students to remove ALL papers from their desk AND backpacks. By order of His Royal Highness, King George III, there will henceforth be a tax of one penny on all written documents in this room. Each student is then responsible for counting up how many of his/her papers have a stamp. This will determine how much his/her tax payment will be at 1 penny per page. Students who do not have the money may use personal property (such as a pencil) to pay their debt. (Note: Keep careful records so payments can be returned after the lesson is over!)

Wearing a crown and with a "kingly voice," the teacher or a student explains to students:
*"I am King George III and any treasonous behavior or language will be punishable by fine, "imprisonment," or both. You should take any complaints or suggestions, as well as your taxes, to the tax collectors. I am unreachable since I am "across the ocean" in Great Britain. My royal tax commissioners will report to me which students are **loyalists**, and which ones are possible **patriots, and thus traitors**."*

King George

(You will need to spend some time explaining these terms and concepts, but as the morning progresses you will hear the students begin to use these words, especially if you and your tax commissioners continue to do so as well.)

During the morning, secretly talk to two or three students. Ask them to be "patriots," and to quietly stir up trouble. They could pass around treasonous letters, hang signs of protest on the walls, secretly form protest groups called the 'Sons of Liberty.' Another thing they could do is "vandalize" a royal tax commissioner's house (desk) by dumping things out on the floor or upsetting his/her chair. Emphasize that whatever they do should not be permanently destructive. Explain that if they are caught by any of the Loyalists or tax commissioners, you, as King George III, will not be able to help them.

If a royal tax commissioner "arrests" a colonist, they should place him/her in a "jail" (a designated area of the room) for a set period. Colonists who are unable to pay their taxes may also need to go to jail. If necessary, you may need to "post" a few British soldiers outside the jail and the Custom's House (place where the tax money is stored). Use other soldiers to help maintain the order in the colony (classroom).

Step 2: Debrief At the end of the morning, spend at least 20 minutes debriefing the experience. Ask students what it felt like to be a loyalist, patriot, British soldier, or royal tax commissioner. Elicit comments about taxation, especially when it is enacted without their representation or votes. You may want to have the students record their experiences in writing. Return their "tax" money, using the tax commissioners written records.

Adapted from a simulation by Diana Parsons, Los Nietos School District.

Activity # 2 Cause and Effect

Using multiple print and digital sources, determine two or more main ideas about the taxes imposed by the British and the reaction of the colonists (RI 5.2).

Share the following Cause and Effect chart with the students. First post the items on the "cause" side and using two or more print or digital sources, have students help fill in the "effect" (RI 5.5).

CAUSE		EFFECT
French and Indian War	**leads to**	**Stamp Act, Townshend Acts**
No colonists vote on taxes	**leads to**	**angry colonists**
Angry colonists	**leads to**	**petitions, boycotts, violence**

Activity #3 Discussion Questions Working in pairs or small groups, have students engage in a range of collaborative discussion questions about the following (SL 5.1):

- Do you think it was the colonists' responsibility to help pay for the French and Indian War? Explain your answer.

- In what different ways did the colonists act against the new taxes?

- Why did the colonists think boycotts might be an effective way to change British attitudes about taxes?

- How might the British have reduced the colonists' anger over the new taxes?

- What is meant by "taxation without representation"?

- Why was the Stamp Act repealed?

- Why did the colonists import more goods than they exported?

- What impact did the presence of British soldiers have on the behavior of the colonists?

- How do individuals and groups today work to make changes in government?

Activity #4 Your Opinion From the point of view of a **loyalist** or a **patriot**, write an opinion piece explaining why the Colonists began to rebel against Great Britain. Introduce the topic, state your opinion, and provide logically organized reasons supported by facts and details. Link your reasons using words, phrases, and clauses (e.g., consequently, specifically). End with a concluding statement or section related to your opinion. (W. 5.1).

Assessment

➤ From the point of view of a **loyalist** or a **patriot**, write an opinion piece explaining why the Colonists began to rebel against Great Britain.

Lesson 3: What was Unfair?

Supporting Question: What disagreements led to the American Revolution?

In this two-day lesson, students explore pre-revolutionary Boston and conflicts that led to the writing of the Declaration of Independence. On Day One, students work in small groups and read and present short plays illustrating historical conflicts between colonists and British authorities. On Day Two, students work in groups to analyze and represent each conflict by creating protest posters to share with the rest of the class.

Day 1 Procedure

Activity # 1 Events That Led to Conflict

Materials needed: Multiple print and digital sources

Using available print and digital sources, help students review events that led to conflict between the British government and American colonists. Cover the following:

Events that Led to Conflict between the British Government and American Colonists

- British and French fought the French and Indian War to decide who rules America.
- The war cost the British a lot of money.
- The British wanted Americans to help pay for the war (Sugar Act, 1764).
- The British imposed new tax laws on Americans.
- The British Parliament passed tax laws without American representation.
- The Americans began to fight British authority by boycotting and smuggling goods and refusing to pay taxes.

Tell students that in the next activity they are going to visit Boston when the British ruled the American colonies. Here, they will explore some of the conflicts that arose between the British government and the American colonies.

Activity # 2 Small Group Activity – Reading Boston Stories

Materials needed: 6 copies of Handouts #3.1, #3.2, #3.3, #3.4 or #3.5 (pages 19 – 23); access to multiple print and digital sources

Divide the class into five groups. Provide copies of a different play (handout) to each group. Each play has five parts. If you have more than five students in a group, assign one student Narrator and another one Expert. Or, divide the script of the Narrator.

Tell students that they are going to read a short play about life in Boston more than 200 years ago. In each play, something unfair happens to a young person.

Step 1: Steps for Students to Follow

- Read the play among yourselves and decide who will play each part.
- Answer the question at the bottom of the play.
- Rehearse your play.

- Present your play to the class as a reader's theater.
- Ask the class to identify what Americans thought was unfair.

While students read and rehearse their plays, circulate among the groups and ask them what they think was unfair in their play. Recommended answers should include the following:

Boston Play #1: British rulers had made taxes without asking the Americans (taxation without representation).
Boston Play #2: British soldiers searched homes and took things that did not belong to them (search and seizure).
Boston Play #3: Americans were told to give food and lodging to British soldiers (quartering act).
Boston Play #4: British rulers did not allow Americans to meet (illegal assembly).
Boston Play #5: American citizens wanted the right to a trial by jury.

Step 2: What Did the Americans Think Was Unfair? Ask each group to present its Boston Play. After each performance, have the Narrator or Expert lead a discussion based on the posted question, **"What did the Americans think was unfair? Why?"**

Collect student handouts. You will need them for Day Two of this lesson. Tell students that in the next class they are going to make posters that protest the unfair things done to people of Boston by King George, the British Parliament, and British soldiers.

Day Two Procedure

Activity # 1 Group Activity – Planning and Drawing Protest Posters

<u>Materials needed</u>: 5 sheets of 12" x 18" white construction paper or unlined chart paper; a variety of colors of felt tip pens; masking tape to hang posters

Explain that as the colonists became angry with British authority, they began to protest. One way they protested was by making posters showing how the British were unfair. These posters were hung in towns and villages so that colonists would learn about the injustices and unite to protest.

Tell students that today they are going to return to Boston where the colonists are becoming more and more angry with British authorities. Explain that now they will have a chance to make their own posters to protest the injustices they experienced in the Boston plays. (You may want to explain that many people in the 13 American colonies suffered unfair treatment at the hands of the British. But British authorities were particularly hard on Boston because they wanted to make it an example to scare all American colonists into obeying British law.)

Divide the class into the same groups as in Day One of this lesson. Redistribute Boston Plays to the appropriate groups.

Distribute paper and drawing supplies and ask students to work together to write a single sentence objecting to an unfair thing that happened in their play.

Tell students they need to use their sentence as a caption somewhere on the poster they draw.

Examples might include:

- Boston Play #1 Do not tax unless you ask.
- Boston Play #2 Our homes belong to us, not you.
- Boston Play #3 No soldiers in our homes. No soldiers at out tables.
- Boston Play #4 We want the right to meet.
- Boston Play #5 We want the right to have a trial by jury.

Activity # 2 Group Activity – Museum Tour
Arrange for groups to display their posters in different areas of the room with group members standing next to their poster.

Explain that each group is going to present its poster to the other groups in a "museum tour." Have each group split into A's and B's. Explain that the A's are first going to be tour guides. The tour guides tell the visiting groups about their poster. The B's will first be the visitors. They will move from poster to poster. Show them the route the B's will take. On a signal have the B's move to the next poster. Give the B's about a minute at each poster and then signal them to move. When the B;'s have seen all of the posters, have them switch roles with the A's and let the A's take the tour.

After the tours, announce that their posters will be on display for several weeks so that everyone can read them. You might refer to the display of posters as the "Democracy Wall."

Important note: Before the next lesson, remove student posters from the display. When the class reassembles, tell them that British authorities have ordered British soldiers to take down all posters that speak out against King George and the British Government.

Assessment
➢ Through the venue of performing a play and creating protest posters, identify what the Americans thought was unfair and why.

Reference: This lesson is adapted from *Adventures in Law and History*, Volume II, "Coming to America, Colonial American, and the Revolutionary Era" Second Edition published by the Constitutional Rights Foundation.

Boston Play #1

Imagine you are living in Boston a long time ago. One day, this happened to you…

Narrator: It is winter in Boston. The year is 1765. The weather is very cold. John and Susan are alone at home. They are playing catch with a ball. Susan throws the ball and John can't get it. It breaks a window. Wind and snow blow inside. Their mother and father will be angry. John and Susan run to the store. Inside the store is the Storekeeper and a British soldier, who is keeping warm by the fire.

Susan: Help! Quick! We need a piece of glass to fix our window.

John: Here is our money.

Storekeeper: You don't have enough money to buy a piece of glass.

Susan: Why not?

Soldier: The Parliament put a tax on glass.

John: What is a tax?

Storekeeper: Extra money you must pay for things that come from Great Britain.

Susan: Why would Parliament do that?

Soldier: We won the war against the French. Now you must help King George pay for the war.

John: That's not fair. **Nobody asked us if we want to help King George pay for the war.**

Storekeeper: Sorry. No tax – no glass. That's the law.

....

Narrator or Expert: What did the Americans think was unfair? Why?

Boston Play #2

Imagine you are living in Boston a long time ago. One day, this happened to you…

Narrator: It is late at night. Everything is quiet in Boston. The year is 1776. Martha is asleep in her attic bedroom. Martha's mother, Anne, is working downstairs. Martha's father is far away, delivering his newspaper to people who live outside Boston. Suddenly there is a loud knocking noise.

British Soldier: Open the door in the name of King George!

Martha: Please don't break down the door. This is our home!

Narrator: Crash! The door breaks open. Two men run into Martha's house.

Anne: Who are you? It is against our laws to enter my home without my permission.

Tax Collector: I am King George's tax collector. I follow the king's laws.

British Soldier: I am a British soldier. I am here to search your house for stolen goods.

Martha: That's against the law. We haven't stolen anything.

British Soldier: I found this bundle of paper hidden in the cellar!

Anne: My husband bought that paper! He uses it to print his newspaper.

Tax Collector: You do not have King George's tax stamp on this paper.

British Soldier: The paper has no tax stamp. We must take it with us.

Martha: That's not fair. **You have broken our laws. They say you can't come into our home and take things that don't belong to you.**

Narrator or Expert: What did the American's think was unfair? Why?

Boston Play #3

Imagine you are living in Boston a long time ago. One day, this happened to you…

Narrator: The time is 1768. The place is Boston, Massachusetts. Nathan and his sister Mary are hungry. The two children spent all morning working hard. Nathan hauled water and Mary boiled it over the kitchen fire. Their mother, Sally, needed hot water to wash Sergeant Jones' dirty uniforms. Sergeant Jones is a British soldier who lives in their home. Now Nathan and Mary sit at the small kitchen table watching Sergeant Jones eat their food.

Sergeant Jones: Both of you look angry. What's wrong with you?

Nathan: We don't have enough food to feed you.

Mary: We don't have enough room for you to live here.

Nathan: We didn't invite you to live in our home.

Sally: You should go back to Great Britain where you belong.

Sergeant Jones: I want to go home. I miss Great Britain.

Mary: So why don't you go home?

Sergeant Jones: I am here to protect you.

Nathan: We don't need protection. The war is over.

Sergeant Jones: What if the French decide to attack Boston?

Mary: You already beat the French.

Sergeant Jones: Here in Boston we are all ruled by King George. He will decide when I can go home.

Sally: It's not fair. **We should not be forced to have soldiers living in our home. We don't have enough food. We don't have enough room in our homes to share with British soldiers.**

● ●

Narrator or Expert: What did the Americans think was unfair? Why?

Boston Play #4

Imagine you are living in Boston a long time ago. One day, this happened to you…

Narrator: The time is 1774. Sarah is walking with her mother and father to the meeting house. The meeting house was a very important place. Here, the people are gathered to talk. Then they would make laws or decide other ways to fix problems in Sarah's town. Sarah wanted to hear her father speak at the meeting house. Her father wanted to speak out against the unfair things that the British soldiers were doing to the people of Boston. At the door of the meeting house, Sarah and her mother and father were stopped by a British soldier.

British Soldier: Halt! The meeting house is closed.

Mothers: Why?

British Soldier: King George has ruled that Americans cannot meet in groups.

Father: Our laws give us the right to meet and make our own decisions.

British Soldier: The people of Boston have broken King George's laws.

Sarah: What laws have we broken?

British Soldier: King George ordered you to pay a tax on tea.

Sarah: But people drink tea every day. We would have to pay a lot of taxes.

Father: Some people in Boston refused to pay the tax. Others poured the tea into the harbor.

Mother: They called this the Boston Tea Party.

British Soldier: Now King George has ordered us to close your meeting halls.

Sarah: But that's not fair. **We have the right to meet and make our own laws.**

....

Narrator or Expert: What did the Americans think was unfair? Why?

Boston Play #5

Imagine you are living in Boston a long time ago. One day, this happened to you…

Narrator: It is January of 1774. Boston is very cold. A British soldier arrested a young boy named Tom Hewes for stealing a loaf of bread. His family is hungry. King George had closed Boston Harbor to punish the people for the Boston Tea Party. Tom's father worked on the docks. Without ships in the harbor there is no work for Tom's father. Without work, there is no money or food for Tom's family. Now Tom was on trial.

British Soldier: Here ye! Here ye! The court of King George is now in session.

Judge: I am the judge of King George's court. What crime has been committed?

British Soldier: Your honor, I caught this boy stealing food from the store of Bess Williams.

Tom Hewes: I am innocent. Bess Williams said I could take the bread.

Judge: Silence, boy! You are a criminal.

Bess Williams: Please, judge. Let a jury decide if this boy is a criminal.

Judge: A British soldier caught this boy stealing. I am a British judge. I will decide if he is innocent or guilty.

Bess Williams: King George closed Boston Harbor. There is no work. People need to eat.

Tom Hewes: I took it for my family. They are hungry.

Bess Williams: Our laws say that a jury made up of people of Boston should decide. They will understand why Tom Hewes took the bread.

Judge: There will be no jury in this case. I will decide if he is guilty or innocent.

Tom Hewes: That's not fair. **I have a right to a trial by jury.**

....

Narrator or Expert: What did the Americans think was unfair? Why?

Lesson 4: The Boston Massacre, 1770

Supporting Question: What were the multiple causes and effects of the Boston Massacre?

Materials needed: a copy of the **Copper Engraving of the Boston Massacre created by Paul Revere** (Handout #4.1, page 28) For a color image, it is highly recommended you go to Google images *Boston Massacre*; and, an enlarged copy of the **Caption on the Engraving of the Boston Massacre** (Handout #4.2, page 29)

Activity # 1 Engraving of the Boston Massacre

Step 1: Boston Massacre Display a copy of the copper engraving **Boston Massacre** created by Paul Revere (Handout #4.1). It is recommended you display a color copy of the engraving. Go to Google images *Boston Massacre*.

Ask students to carefully look at the engraving as they answer questions such as:

- What do you see happening in this engraving? Take turns mentioning whatever you see happening, no matter how small. Look at the <u>people</u> (their facial expressions, poses, gestures, clothing). Look at the <u>activities.</u> (What are the people doing?) What <u>objects</u> do you see in the picture?

- What is the setting of this picture? (Where does it take place?) What historical period is this? What do you see in the picture that makes you think that?

- Why do you think Paul Revere created this engraving? What was he trying to tell us about the people, the place, and life during this time? What ideas and/or emotions do you think this work of art expresses? How does it make you feel about the people in the engraving?

- Write a caption to go with this engraving that tells what you think Paul Revere wanted people to know. What would you have called this work of art if you had made it yourself?

- What are some questions that you would like to ask the artist about his work?

Step 2: Caption Display the caption that Paul Revere wrote above the engraving (Handout #4.2). Read the caption to students:

"THE FRUITS OF ARBITRARY POWER, OR THE BLOODY MASSACRE, PERPETRATED IN KING STREET BOSTON MARCH 5, 1770, ON WHICH MESS.RS.SAML GRAY, SAML MAVERICK, JAMES CALDWELL, CRISPUS ATTUCKS, PATRICK CARR WERE KILLED, SIX OTHER WOUNDED TWO OF THEM MORTALLY"

Step 3: Ask Questions
- What new information do we now have about the engraving? Date? Location?

- Who do you think the people are who were killed or wounded? What makes you think that?

- Loaded words are words that are emotionally charged. Which words in this writing are loaded? What does Revere mean by, "THE FRUITS OF ARBITRARY POWER?" How do the words "BLOODY MASSACRE" make you feel? Why would Revere use loaded words?

Activity # 2 Analyzing the Artist's work: The Boston Massacre

As students continue to view the engraving, explain the following artistic terms:

Composition – The figures and action are in the **foreground** while the buildings are the **background**. The foreground has two distinct groups, joined by the smoke from the Redcoat's muskets. As the Redcoats advance from right to left, the colonists fall back in disarray. The viewer sees the scene from a central vantage point.

Mood – The emphasis is on the orderliness of the British as contrasted to the defenseless colonists. The brutality of the attack is underscored by the placement of the mortally wounded in the foreground.

Color and Line – Ivory-toned buildings form a neutral backdrop for the foreground scene. British red coats, black boots and hats stand out boldly while civilian clothes blend with the background. Figures are crudely drawn with mask-like features and large heads.

Activity # 3 Read to students the following background information.

In 1767, Parliament passed the Townshend Acts which levied taxes on British imports in America such as paper, glass, lead, paints, and tea, the most popular beverage in America. The colonists objected to the taxes imposed on them by the British Parliament. "Taxation without representation is tyranny!" became the angry cry. The Americans resisted and organized a boycott of imports from England. Even the British merchants began to protest because they were losing money. Britain stationed troops in several colonies to help keep order – and that led to more trouble. Parliament finally gave in and repealed the taxes, except for the tea tax.

The people of Boston hated having the British soldiers in their city. They felt they could defend themselves without help. On March 5, 1770, things got totally out of control. Snow had fallen that day until noon. British soldiers, called Redcoats because of the color of their uniform, were guarding Boston's Customs House. This is where the tax money was stored.

An unruly crowd of about four hundred men had collected in front of the Customs House. They shouted at the soldiers and called them "lobsters" and "bloody backs" because of their red uniforms. By evening, the soldiers were ill-tempered because the townspeople had been insulting them more than usual, throwing rocks and snowballs at them; and pressing up close to the muzzles of their guns, daring them to fire.

The solitary sentry called for help. Captain Preston and seven privates came to his rescue, but the people were not afraid of nine British soldiers. Then someone – it was never clear who – actually did shout, "FIRE!" Others said they heard, "Hold your fire!"

The frightened soldiers panicked and leveled their muskets and pulled the triggers. Five men were killed, and six were wounded. One of the victims, Crispus Attucks, was reportedly the first colonist killed. Attucks was a 47-year old African American former slave and a member of the Sons of Liberty.

Activity # 4 Put Yourself in the Picture.

Step 1: Imagine you are there in Boston on March 5, 1770. Ask students some of the following questions to help them imagine what it was like to be a part of the Boston Massacre.

- What sounds do you hear and what smells are there?
- Where are you standing or sitting or lying in the scene? What is surrounding you? (Have some students describe where they are, and other students can guess their location in the picture.)
- What is the temperature? Is it warm, hot, cool, cold? How do you know?
- What are you doing? Adopt the facial expression, pose, and gesture of the person in the picture. (Students can guess which people they are depicting based on their poses, etc.)
- What are you wearing and/or holding? How does your clothing feel?
- What objects are around you? Why are they there? What are they used for?
- Who else is with you? What are they doing?
- What were all of you doing five minutes before this scene?
- What are you going to do next? What will the scene look like in the next moment?

Step 2: Discussion Questions Discuss the following questions with students (SL 5.6)

- Does Revere depict a point of view that is favorable to the British soldiers or to the colonists? Why?
- If a British artist illustrated the Boston Massacre, how might it look different?

Activity # 5 What Happened Next?

Read to students the following information about what happened next?

The fight at the Customs House was reported throughout the colonies. Samuel Adams wrote articles about the event, exaggerating the details and calling it the Boston Massacre. Paul Revere made an engraving of the massacre with the soldiers all in a line firing their guns at peaceful citizens. Revere knew that the picture did not accurately tell the facts about what happened in Boston. The British soldiers did not stand right in front of the colonists and shoot them, but Revere wanted to stir up hatred for the British. Thousands of copies were printed and circulated all over the colonies. This powerful piece of propaganda helped to spread the news and ignite the anger of the colonists even more.

To avoid further trouble, the British pulled their troops out of Boston and stationed them at a nearby harbor fort. The eight soldiers who had fired their muskets were arrested and tried for murder. They were defended by a Massachusetts lawyer, John Adams who later became the first vice president and the second president of the United States. Adams hated the presence of British troops, but he also believed that the soldiers had a right to protect themselves and were entitled to a fair trial. Adams argued in court that they had defended themselves against a lawless mob. Six of the defendants were acquitted. The other two were convicted of manslaughter, a lesser offense than murder. They were branded on their thumbs and released.

Assessment

> ➢ Pose relevant questions about the events pictured in the engraving of the Boston Massacre created by Paul Revere.
> ➢ Identify and interpret the multiple causes and effects of the Boston Massacre.

Extended Activities

Before, During, and After

Invite students to act out, draw images, or write paragraphs that describe what happened just before the Boston Massacre, during the conflict, and the next scene or sequence of events. If desired, have different students take on the perspective of the colonial patriots and the British soldiers.

Mock Trail

Conduct a mock trial to determine what "really" happened. Have students take the part of a British soldier and a patriot with others serving as prosecutor, defense attorney and judge. The remaining students serve as the jury, but they can also ask questions.

Developing Writing Skills
Activity developed by Dr. Rhoda Coleman

Help students expand their writing skills by creating some sample sentences together. To teach "COMPARE AND CONTRAST," model "HOWEVER" sentences, including the use of commas. For example, "The British wore uniforms, however, the Patriots did not." What other HOWEVER sentence can you create to go with the engraving?

To teach "CAUSE AND EFFECT," model how to write "BECAUSE" sentences from the point of view of the person on whom they are reporting. For example, "The British fired because the crowd threw things at them." Or "Because the crowd threw things at them, the British fired on them." Work together to create more BECAUSE sentences to show cause and effect relationships.

To help students write a DIALOGUE to go with the engraving, brainstorm together a list of words that can be used instead of "said." For example, "Don't shoot!" shouted Captain Preston. Note how the word "shouted" is much more powerful than "said." This is also a good opportunity to help students learn how to punctuate sentences that use direct quotations. Possible substitutes for "said" include:

accused	growled	quarreled
argued	harangued	scoffed
badgered	insinuated	sneered
blamed	jeered	taunted
bullied	ordered	urged
demanded	pestered	yelled
exaggerated	proclaimed	

Copper Engraving of the Boston Massacre
Created by Paul Revere

Note: It is highly recommended you display a color copy of this image from a reference such as: Google Images *Boston Massacre.*

Caption on the Engraving of the Boston Massacre

"THE FRUITS OF ARBITRARY POWER, OR THE BLOODY MASSACRE, PERPETRATED IN KING STREET BOSTON MARCH 5, 1770, ON WHICH MESS.RS.SAML GRAY, SAML MAVERICK, JAMES CALDWELL, CRISPUS ATTUCKS, PATRICK CARR WERE KILLED, SIX OTHER WOUNDED TWO OF THEM MORTALLY"

Lesson 5: The Boston Tea Party
and the Coercive Acts

Supporting Questions
- Why did the Sons of Liberty dump crates of British tea into Boston Harbor?
- What was the British response to the Boston Tea Party?
- How effective was the Boston Tea Party?

Activity # 1 Four Corners

Materials needed: For each student, a copy of **Four Corners** (Handout #5.1, pages 33-34); a set of signs, one for each corner of the classroom. Each sign should read one of the following: The East India Tea Company, Broadsides, The Boston Tea Party, and The Coercive (Intolerable) Acts; 4 sets of Discussion Socks (pairs of socks rolled up to form a ball) or beanbags.

Step 1: Discussion Socks Show the Discussion Socks (or bean bags) and explain that after silently reading a short selection, there will be several Discussion Questions. When discussing a question, only the person holding the Discussion Sock may speak, no one else may interrupt. When the person is finished speaking, other students who wish to speak may raise their hand and the Discussion Sock may be softly tossed to a student whose hand is raised. No one may have the discussion sock again until all students have had a chance to speak.

Step 2: Select Your Corner Post one of the following topics in each corner of the classroom: The East India Tea Company, Broadsides, The Boston Tea Party, and The Coercive (Intolerable) Acts.

Present the four related topics to the whole group and give the students some "think time."

Explain the following steps:
- Choose a corner of your choice and move to the respective corner. If one corner is too crowded, move to a different corner.
- Silently read the selection for your corner. Circle any unknown words. After reading, discuss the words within your group. Reread the selection and underline important ideas.
- Using the Discussion Sock, respond to the discussion questions by making comments that contribute to the discussion and elaborate on the remarks of others (SL 5.1).
- When finished, representatives from each corner share what their group discussed.

Corner #1:

The East India Tea Company

British merchants established a tea trading company in India and by 1773 the East India Company was near **bankruptcy**. The company convinced Parliament to pass the Tea Act granting them a **monopoly** in the colonial tea trade. The special privileges granted the British East India Company actually lowered the price colonists had to pay for tea. The colonists protested the tea tax and refused to purchase the tea, even if the price was lower, because it meant that they would be paying the tax imposed by Parliament.

Discussion Questions:
- What does it mean when a company is "near bankruptcy?" What kinds of things might a company do if it thinks it might go out of business? (lower its prices, try to get help)
- What does it mean to have a "monopoly" on the tea trade? (a monopoly means exclusive control by one group) Why was this a problem? (no choice)
- Why did the colonists protest the monopoly granted to the East India Company when it meant lower prices on the tea? (They didn't want to pay the tax.)
- What choices did the colonists have? (protest the tea tax, give up drinking tea, smuggle tea in from somewhere else)

Corner #2

> ## Broadsides
>
> The British tea ship *Dartmouth* docked at Griffin's Wharf in Boston on November 28, 1773. The next morning, the town was plastered with broadsides. A broadside is a large sheet of paper, usually written on one side, that contains an advertisement or public notice.
>
> **Friends! Brethren! Countrymen! That worst Plagues, the detested tea shipped for this port by the East India Company, is now arrived in the Harbour; the hour of destruction or manly opposition to…Tyranny, stares you in the Face.**

Discussion Questions:

- Who do you think wrote the broadsides and what was their problem?
- What actions do the broadsides want to be taken?
- What other actions could the writers of the broads have taken?
- What actions do people take today when there is something they do not like?

Corner #3

> ## The Boston Tea Party
>
> Two more ships, the *Beaver* and the *Eleanor* soon joined the *Dartmouth*. Protesters demanded the ships return to London with their cargoes. A mass meeting was held on December 16, 1773 at Boston's Old South Church. The meeting ended when the Sons of Liberty, disguised as Mohawk Indians, boarded the English ships and dumped their entire cargo of 342 chests of tea into Boston Harbor.

Discussion Questions:
- What did the patriots hope to accomplish by throwing the tea into Boston Harbor?
- Were the protestors justified in dumping the tea into the harbor? Why or why not?
- What other measures could the people of Boston have taken?
- What actions can Americans take today if there is a law they don't like?

Corner #4

> ## The Coercive Acts
>
> When news of the Boston Tea Party finally reached England, King George was furious. He demanded the colonists be punished for their behavior. They must be taught a lesson. To punish Massachusetts for the Tea Party, Parliament passed a series of laws called the **Coercive Acts**. The laws said no ship carrying colonial goods could leave Boston Harbor

until the colonists had paid for all the tea that was destroyed. To enforce the new law, Parliament ordered the Royal Navy to **blockade** the harbor to prevent ships from leaving or entering. Thousands more soldiers were sent to Boston. The British government also forbid town meetings, except for one each year. And, they ordered the colonists to **quarter** British soldiers. This meant they had to feed the soldiers and give them a place to sleep. These Coercive Acts were known throughout the colonies as the "**Intolerable Acts**." They united colonial opposition to the British from Massachusetts to Georgia.

Discussion Questions:
- How did the British respond to the Boston Tea Party? Why did the British feel such harsh measures were necessary against Boston?
- Why did the colonists call the restrictions (Coercive Acts) "intolerable acts?"
- Would the Sons of Liberty have gone through with the "tea party" had they suspected it would result in such restrictive measures as the Intolerable Acts?
- How effective was the Boston Tea Party?
- Analyze why some colonists remained loyal to the king while others rebelled against him.

Step 3: Read and Share As a class, read each of the four reading selections. Have group members who read the text quote from the text the important ideas they underlined and take turns sharing their answers to the discussion questions (RI 5.1).

Activity #2 Boston Tea Party

Step 1: Find Out More Working with a partner, students use multiple print and digital sources to learn more about different aspects of the Boston Tea Party:
1. Who organized the Tea Party?
2. Whose idea was it to dump the tea?
3. Why did the participants wear disguises?
4. How much tea was dumped?
5. How effective was the Tea Party?

Step 2: Write About It – Take Your Pick With your partner, select one of the following writing projects (W 5.7). Your task is to create a:

- Tea Party Blog (include multiple entries)
- Tea Party Board Game
- Newspaper Article about the Boston Tea Party
- Tea Party Poem or Song
- Tea Party Reader's Theater or Script, including characters and a narrator

Each writing project must:
- include responses to the five questions you researched in Step 1
- demonstrate an in-depth understanding of the historical content
- support all main ideas with accurate facts
- contain substantial supportive evidence

Assessment
➢ With a partner, tell about different aspects of the Tea Party by creating a blog, board game, newspaper article, poem or song, or a Reader's Theater.

Select Your Corner

Corner #1

The East India Tea Company

British merchants established a tea trading company in India and by 1773 the East India Company was near bankruptcy. The company convinced Parliament to pass the Tea Act granting them a monopoly in the colonial tea trade. The special privileges granted the British East India Company actually lowered the price colonists had to pay for tea. The colonists protested the tea tax and refused to purchase the tea, even if the price was lower, because it meant that they would be paying the tax imposed by Parliament.

Discussion Questions:

- What does it mean when a company is "near bankruptcy?" What kinds of things might a company do if it thinks it might go out of business?

- What does it mean to have a "monopoly" on the tea trade? (a monopoly means exclusive control by one group) Why was this a problem?

- Why did the colonists protest the monopoly granted to the East India Company when it meant lower prices on the tea?

- What choices did the colonists have?

Corner #2:

Broadsides

The British tea ship *Dartmouth* docked at Griffin's Wharf in Boston on November 28, 1773. The next morning, the town was plastered with broadsides. A broadside is a large sheet of paper, usually written on one side, that contains an advertisement or public notice.

Friends! Brethren! Countrymen! That worst Plagues, the detested tea shipped for this port by the East India Company, is now arrived in the Harbour; the hour of destruction or manly opposition to…Tyranny, stares you in the Face.

Discussion Questions:

- Who do you think wrote the broadsides and what was their problem?
- What actions do the broadsides want to be taken?
- What other actions could the writers of the broads have taken?
- What actions do people take today when there is something they do not like?

Corner #3:

The Boston Tea Party

Two more ships, the *Beaver* and the *Eleanor* soon joined the *Dartmouth*. Protesters demanded the ships return to London with their cargoes. A mass meeting was held on December 16, 1773 at Boston's Old South Church. The meeting ended when the Sons of Liberty, disguised as Mohawk Indians, boarded the English ships and dumped their entire cargo of 342 chests of tea into Boston Harbor.

Discussion Questions:

- What did the patriots hope to accomplish by throwing the tea into Boston Harbor?

- Were the protestors justified in dumping the tea into the harbor? Why or why not?

- What other measures could the people of Boston have taken?
- What actions can Americans take today if there is a law they do not like?

Corner #4:

The Coercive Acts

When news of the Boston Tea Party finally reached England, King George was furious. He demanded the colonists be punished for their behavior. They must be taught a lesson. To punish Massachusetts for the Boston Tea Party, Parliament passed a series of laws called the **Coercive Acts**. The laws said no ship carrying colonial goods could leave Boston Harbor until the colonists had paid for all the tea that was destroyed. To enforce the new law, Parliament ordered the Royal Navy to **blockade** the harbor to prevent ships from leaving or entering. Thousands more soldiers were sent to Boston.

The British government also forbid town meetings, except for one each year. And, they ordered the colonists to **quarter** British soldiers. This meant they had to feed the soldiers and give them a place to sleep. These Coercive Acts were known throughout the colonies as the "**Intolerable Acts**." They united colonial opposition to the British from Massachusetts to Georgia.

Discussion Questions:

- How did the British respond to the Boston Tea Party? Why did the British feel such harsh measures were necessary against Boston?

- Why did the colonists call the restrictions (Coercive Acts) "intolerable acts?"

- Would the Sons of Liberty have gone through with the "tea party" had they suspected it would result in such restrictive measures as the Intolerable Acts?

- How effective was the Boston Tea Party?
- Analyze why some colonists remained loyal to the king while others rebelled against him.

Lesson 6: Katie's Trunk

Supporting Question: What happened to a family who remained loyal to England?

Materials needed: a copy of the book *Katie's Trunk*; picture of a trunk (from the title page of the book); picture of Katie crawling into the trunk (page 17 of the book); for each student, a copy of **Vocabulary Cards** (Handout #6.1, page 37); chart paper with the decision tree outline.

Summary: The story *Katie's Trunk* takes place during the Revolutionary War. A young girl named Katie faces rejection from her former peers and neighbors because of being a Loyalist (Tory). When the rebels come to ransack her home for money and valuables, Katie and her family hide in the nearby forest. Angered by what is happening, Katie returns to her home and hides from the rebels in her mother's wedding trunk. When the mob begins to search the trunk, a neighbor of Katie's discovers that she is there but doesn't tell his companions. Instead, he frightens them away and leaves the trunk open so she can breathe. *Katie's Trunk* gives a thought-provoking glimpse of the beginnings of the American Revolution. It shows a community being torn apart by the Revolution.

Activity #1 *Katie's Trunk*

Step 1: Trunk Show a picture of a trunk. Begin by asking the children what the name of this object is. Ask, "What would you put in there? What things could have been stored in those trunks during the Revolutionary War?"

Step 2: Academic Vocabulary Discuss the following vocabulary words so students may have a greater understanding of what the words mean when you come to them in the story (Refer to Handout #6.1).

- "these letters your papa speaks of" refers to the letters from a farmer in Pennsylvania to the inhabitants of the British Colonies. Originally published in a newspaper, this widely reproduced pamphlet by John Dickinson declared that Parliament could not tax the colonies and it called the Townshend Acts unconstitutional.
- "that tea they dumped in the harbor" This phrase refers to the Boston Tea Party. When British tea ships arrived in Boston Harbor, many citizens wanted the tea sent back to England without the payment of any taxes. The royal governor insisted on payment of all taxes. On December 16, 1773, a group of men disguised as Mohawk Indians boarded the ships and dumped all the tea in Boston Harbor.
- a "Tory" means a Loyalist, or someone who remained loyal to the British king
- a "Rebel" means a Patriot, or a colonist who was against British rule and supported the rebel cause in the American colonies
- a "parlor" is a room in a private home set apart for the entertainment of visitors; a small room
- "English goods" refers to any items made in England
- a "skirmish" is a minor battle in a war

Step 3: Katie's Trunk By the raise of hands, have the students indicate if they have ever had someone stop liking them for something they did not really do.

Tell students that you are going to read them a story about a little girl who had her friends stop liking her just because of something she and her family believe. This story is based on a true story that happened to the author's ancestor.

Read *Katie's Trunk* until page 12 in the book. Stop after "I raced for the house, Mama's fierce whisper trying to call me back."

Step 4: Make a Decision Display the **decision tree chart paper** with the two choices being "staying with family" and "returning to house." Tell students they are going to think about Katie's choices and her decision whether to go back to the house. Working with suggestions from the students, fill out the decision tree. Ask students to explain and defend their answers. Discuss which course of action the students think is the best one to follow. Possible answers:

Choice # 1 Staying with Family	Choice # 2 Returning to house
Good Consequences	**Good Consequences**
stay safe, protect family, don't give away the hiding place	hide valuables, scare away robbers, convince them to leave peacefully
Bad Consequences	**Bad Consequences**
no one to protect home, home could be destroyed, rebels get money for war	captured, killed, injured, can't stop rebels, family will be worried

Step 5: Trunk Show students the picture of Katie climbing in her mother's trunk. Ask them what would make Katie hide in the trunk? Tell them about a few things that took place during the Revolutionary War. For example, the rebels sometimes stole "English goods" from Loyalists and sold them to raise money to buy guns and ammunition.

Read the rest of the story. After reading the book, ask students, "What do you think will happen next?" Explain that during the Revolutionary War, neighbor often fought against neighbor and friends fought against a former friend.

Tell students that we will be learning more about the Revolutionary War. Katie's family members are **loyalists** to the King of England. In the next lesson we will learn about some **patriots** who do not think the policies of the King of England are fair.

Activity #2 Reader's Theater for *Katie's Trunk*

Materials needed: 7 copies of Reader's Theater for *Katie's Trunk* (Handout #6.2 page 38).

Select seven students to play the roles of Katie, Mama, Papa, Walter, Celia Warren, Reuben Otis, and John Warren. Students each sit in a chair in the front of the room. If desired, select six easy costumes the children can wear to portray the character they are representing. It is helpful to number the pages in the book *Katie's Trunk* beginning with page 1 of the story.

For each of the 7 characters, provide the script below. The teacher becomes the Narrator and reads the story stopping at each set of quotation marks for the character to say his or her lines. The underlined section is the "cue" to the character that he/she will speak after these words are read by the narrator. The person in the parentheses speaks the lines.

Assessment
➤ Identify good and bad consequences of Katie's decision to return to her home.
➤ Selected students participate in a Reader's Theater (Optional).

    Vocabulary Cards for *Katie's Trunk*

"these letters your papa speaks of" refers to the letters from a farmer in Pennsylvania to the inhabitants of the British Colonies. Originally published in a newspaper, this widely reproduced pamphlet by John Dickinson declared that Parliament could not tax the colonies and it called the Townshend Acts unconstitutional.

"that tea they dumped in the harbor" This phrase refers to the Boston Tea Party. When British tea ships arrived in Boston Harbor, many citizens wanted the tea sent back to England without the payment of any taxes. The royal governor insisted on payment of all taxes. On December 16, 1773, a group of men disguised as Mohawk Indians boarded the ships and dumped all the tea in Boston Harbor.

a **"Tory"** means a **Loyalist**, or someone who remained loyal to the British king

a **"Rebel"** means a **Patriot**, or a colonist who was against British rule and supported the rebel cause in the American colonies

a **"parlor"** is a room in a private home set apart for the entertainment of visitors; a small room

"English goods" refers to any items made in England

a **"skirmish"** is a minor battle in a war

         Reader's Theater for *Katie's Trunk*

Listen carefully for the underlined words. This is the signal to read your lines immediately afterward.

Page 1: (Mama) <u>Mama sighed and said</u>, "I should sit you down to sew seams all day and get the goodness straight inside, Katie. What is wrong with you?"

Page 3 (Mama) <u>Mama sighed and sat down to tea</u>. "Must be all this trouble and fighting. Why it makes me skittish as a newborn calf, all this marching and talking, these letters your Papa speaks of, that tea they dumped in the harbor."

Page 4 (Mama) <u>Mama's hand shook</u>. "Tea! In the Harbor!" Wasting God's good food."

(Walter) <u>Brother Walter said</u> "That's not the least of it. It will get worse."

(Mama) <u>She peered at him</u>. "How could it get worse, Walter?"

Page 7 (Celia Warren) <u>Sometimes I heard that word hissed</u> "Tory!"

Page 8 (Papa) <u>Papa came running</u>. "Get your mother! Hide in the woods. The rebels are coming."

Page 15 (Reuben) <u>Then I heard voices by the door, Reuben Otis, John Warren, Harold Smith and others, not our neighbors.</u> "This'll be fine pickings!"

Pages 17-18 (Reuben) <u>Their footsteps next door in the parlor</u>. "English goods!"

Page 18 (Reuben) <u>I heard Reuben say</u>, "Mr. Gray has money here. Look hard for it."

Page 21 (Katie) <u>I thought my words might go up to God like bubbles in a pond to the silver top where they would burst</u>. "Please, God, don't let them find me, don't let them hurt us, let me breathe."

(John Warren) <u>There was not enough air.</u> "Fine dresses and silver here."

(John Warren) <u>Maybe he didn't know. Suddenly he shouted</u>, "Out! The Tories are coming. Back to the road! Hurry!"

Page 24 (Mama) <u>Only Mama scolded</u>, "Katie! Leaving us that way…"

(Papa) <u>Papa looked out the window</u>. "It's not bad, dear ones, just a skirmish. No one's hurt that I can see."

Lesson 7: The Role of Colonial Women
During the American Revolution

Supporting Questions
- What different roles did women play during the American Revolution?
- What were the trade-offs and opportunity costs in the decision to boycott British goods?

Activity # 1 The Role of Colonial Women

Materials needed: For each student, a copy of **Key Women During the American Revolution** (Handout # 7.1, page 41).

Step 1: Women Played an Active Part in the American Revolution Ask students to predict, "What roles do you think the women played in the American Revolution?"

Background information: Colonial women found a variety of ways to participate in the protest movement against the British. They boycotted tea. To **boycott** means to stop buying or using the goods or services of a certain company or country as a protest; the noun **boycott** is the protest itself. They also boycotted British-made clothing (RI 5.6).

They spun thread and made cloth for soldier's uniforms. The women cared for the farm and family back home while the men were fighting, and they followed the men and the army to help with the cooking and laundry and tend to the injured. Some women went so far as to serve as spies or to disguise themselves as men in order to fight.

Step 2: Key Women During the American Revolution Who were some of the key women of the Revolutionary War era? Place students into five groups, one for each of the following women: Martha Washington, Abigail Adams, Mercy Otis Warren, Phillis Wheatley, and Mary Hays ("Molly Pitcher").

Provide students with a copy of the Key Women During the American Revolution (Handout # 7.1). Assign each group one of the women to read about and, when finished, report their findings to the class by providing two or more main ideas from the text about the role the woman played in the American Revolution and explaining how this is supported by key details in the text (RI 5.2).

If time allows, have students in each group do further research about the women. Using a variety of print and digital sources, they should analyze multiple accounts of the same woman, noting similarities and differences in the point of view they represent (RI 5.6).

Recommended website: https://revolutionarywomengroup6.weebly.com/african-american-women.html Women in the American Revolution. Review the tabs for Gender Issues, Literary Ladies (Adams and Wheatley), African American Women in the American Revolution (Wheatley), and Women and the Army (Deborah Sampson).

The Washington Letter to Wheatley, February 28, 1776, is in the National Digital Library (Library of Congress) collection of the Washington Papers. A transcription is online at https://founders.archives.gov/documents/Washington/03-03-02-0281.

Activity # 2 Making Economic Choices

Background Information: Women did not take to the streets fighting, but they did make their views known by banding together in societies called the Daughters of Liberty.

When Parliament levied taxes on British imports such as British-made cloth, the women had difficult **economic choices** to make. When you buy something, you are making an economic choice. When you buy or do one thing, you give up buying or doing something else. This is called a **trade-off**. What you give up is called the **opportunity cost** (RI 5.4).

Should you continue to purchase the beautiful, fine-woven British cloth or should you do without? Colonial Women had to decide what was more important to them, fine clothes or showing their resentment toward England. The colonists were angry about the tax so many **boycotted** or refused to buy anything made in England (RI 5.4).

What happened? Many of the women stopped wearing dresses made from British cloth and gathered in churches, courthouses, and meeting halls to spin and weave their own cloth. This sturdy homespun cloth became the patriotic fashion.

Clothing was in short supply after the blockade of Boston Harbor, so the Patriot women worked at their spinning wheels and land looms to make homespun coats for the Continental Army. The British soldiers would make fun of Washington's troops by calling them "homespuns."

Discussion Question: Why did the colonists think **boycotts** might be an effective way to change British attitudes about taxes?

Activity # 3: Diary and Journal Writing
Explain that a diary is a book where you record personal thoughts about your life, the people in it, and the things you care about. A diary is for you and by you. Your diary is a safe place where you can be honest about your thoughts, feelings and opinions. A diary can tell about events as they happen, and it can tell about dreams you have. Today we often think of girls as writing diaries; however, from the seventeenth century, when diaries came into being, most well-known diarists were men. Today, men often write journals where they can communicate in private the highs, lows and all their emotions in between. Journals are a safe place to offload without the fear of being judged. Journaling helps you prioritize your problems, fears, and concerns. It is simply writing down your thoughts and feelings to understand them more clearly.

Prompt: Option 1-Select one of the Colonial women during the Revolutionary War and write at least 3 diary entries as if you are her. Date your diary entry, begin your entry "Dear Diary," and tell about your daily experiences and your thoughts. Option 2-select one of the people listed on page 8 of this guide and write at least three journal entries for him/her (W 5.3)

Note: Before writing, use multiple print and digital resources to research the person so you can write the diary or journal from their viewpoint using accurate, descriptive details.

Assessment

- In a group, read about and then orally report their findings to the class providing two or more main ideas from the text how this is supported by key details in the text
- Using accurate, descriptive details, write at least three diary or journal entries from the viewpoint of a Colonial person during the Revolutionary War.

Key Women During the American Revolution

Sometimes, families traveled with their men and the army. The armies did not fight in the winter so General George Washington's wife, **Martha Washington** (1731-1802), spent eight years in winter camp with her husband, returning to Mount Vernon, their Virginia home, each spring. Few letters or documents describe Martha's experiences the winter at Valley Forge, but she was kept busy managing the servants, ordering supplies, entertaining officers' wives, organizing dinners, and running the household, freeing her husband to concentrate on military matters. A widow, Martha Dandridge Custis had married George Washington on January 6, 1759. He took over as father to her son, Jacky, and her daughter, Patsy.

Abigail Adams (1744-1818) ran the family farm in Massachusetts while husband John was working in the Continental Congress in Philadelphia. One of the first supporters of women's rights, she wrote letters to her husband, reminding him, "...remember the ladies, and be more generous and favorable to them than your ancestors..." From her letters, we can learn about the customs, the issues, the events and day-to-day family life of the Revolutionary War era. Like other women of the time, Abigail had no formal schooling, but she read widely and spoke her mind freely. Abigail was the wife of the second president of the United States, John Adams, and the mother of John Quincy Adams, the sixth president. What other woman is also the wife and the mother of U.S. Presidents? (Barbara Bush)

Mercy Otis Warren (1728-1814) was known by many as the "First Lady of the Revolution." (Her brother, James Otis, was the colonist who said "no taxation without representation" as he urged his fellow colonists to not buy paper goods that had been stamped.) Mercy Otis Warren wrote plays that made fun of the British. She was a friend of many leaders of the revolution. Printed in pamphlets, her plays were very popular. Later, she wrote three books that described the American Revolution.

Phillis Wheatley (1753-1784) came to Boston on a slave ship when she was eight years old. Phillis was bought by John and Susannah Wheatley. They taught her, unlike other slaves, to speak English and to read and write. She loved to write poetry and is known as the first published African American woman poet. Her first book of poems was published in London in 1773. She was only the second woman in America to have her poems published in a book. Some very famous Americans like Benjamin Franklin, John Hancock, and George Washington read her poems. During the Revolutionary War, Phillis wrote a poem praising George Washington as the Commander of the army and sent him a copy. Washington liked the poem wrote a letter to Phillis asking if she came to Cambridge please stop to see him.

The Battle of Monmouth was only one of the many confrontations between American and British forces. **Mary Hays** (1754-1832) carried pitchers of water to the thirsty troops and to cool down the cannons. This earned her the nickname of "**Molly Pitcher**." On June 28, 1778, some historians also credit her with taking over her husband's job loading and firing a cannon after he was wounded in battle. After the war she was awarded a pension of forty dollars a year for her service. Molly Pitcher has become an American folk hero, but little is really known about her. Private Joseph Martin wrote the only eyewitness account of Mary Hay's bravery at the Battle of Monmouth.

Lesson 8: *The Declaration of Independence*

Supporting Question

What is the Declaration of Independence and how did it mark the creation of a new nation?

Activity # 1 Academic Vocabulary

<u>Materials needed</u>: For each group of 3 or 4 students, a copy of the **Cut and Sort Vocabulary Cards** (Handout #8.1, page 44) and **Vocabulary for the Story of the Declaration of Independence** (Handout #8.2, page 45)

Step 1: Vocabulary Cards Divide the students into groups of 4. Give each group a copy of the Cut and Sort Vocabulary Cards (Handout #8.1). Group members cut apart the vocabulary cards and group them into three piles: "Colonies," "Great Britain" or "Can't Tell."

Step 2: Re-sort the Vocabulary Cards Distribute a copy of Vocabulary for the Story of the Declaration of Independence (Handout #8.2). Using this new information, have students re-sort the vocabulary cards. Each group shares their groupings and, depending on their reasoning or evidence, many words could be listed as either "Colonies" or "Great Britain" (RI 5.6 and SL 5.3).

colonies – lands or provinces that are far away from a country that rules over them

settlement – place where people make their permanent homes

Great Britain - island nation west of Europe made up originally of three older countries, England, Scotland, Wales and led by a King or Queen and Parliament

colonists – the people who live in the colonies

Parliament – the legislature of the British government

representatives – people who are chosen to speak for others from their community, colony or state

patriot – one who loves a country

taxes – money that governments collect from people or from the sale of goods to help pay the costs of government

Redcoats – British soldiers, who wore red uniforms

intolerable – describes something so bad that a person cannot live with it

Minutemen – armed civilians who pledged to be ready in a minute to defend their communities from attack

Continental Congress – gathering of representatives from the 13 colonies of British North America to decide colonial plans and policy

legislature – the part of a government that is made up of people elected to make rules and set taxes

ignore – pay no attention to

draft – to write an early version of something, or the version itself

declaration – announcement or full statement

independence – separateness, ability to stand on one's own

rights – the powers and opportunities a person or group should be able to get

parchment –a piece of animal skin treated to become a good, long-lasting surface for writing

pamphleteer – one who writes a pamphlet, or short booklet, on a single subject

Activity # 2 The Story of the Declaration of Independence

<u>Materials needed</u>: For each pair of students, a copy of **"The Story of the Declaration of Independence"** (Handout #8.3, pages 46-48); scissors; map of the original 13 colonies; multiple print and digital sources

Step 1: Story Handout #8.3 is a retelling of "The Story of the Declaration of Independence." Depending on the needs of your students, **break up the story into several parts over 2 days**. As you read, have students find the locations mentioned on a map.

Vocabulary words from Activity #1 are written in bold in the text. Have students number the paragraphs of the text. It is recommended you use the 3-Step process for Close Reading.

- Read the text to get the "gist" or rough idea of it. Circle unknown words (RI 5.2).
- Read the text again slowing down to make annotations and clarify unknown words. What is the text structure – description, problem and solution, compare and contrast, cause and effect, sequence (dates over time) (RI 5.4, 5.5, 5.6).
- Read through the lens of a specific purpose, find and underline supporting evidence. Is the author's purpose to **P**ersuade, **I**nform, or **E**ntertain? "It's as easy as **PIE**" (RI 5.8).

Close Reading suggestions from Kirsten Hill, Desert Sands Unified School District

Step 2: Discussion Questions
- What is the author's message in this text?

- What were the ties between British people and Americans from the start of the colonies' settlement?

- What happened that made the colonies' representatives in Philadelphia feel that making the colonies a separate country was a good idea?

- Why do we celebrate the Fourth of July?

Share with the students that the Founders' patriotism for their country was deep and profound. By signing the Declaration of Independence, those men were signing their own "death warrants," as Benjamin Rush, one of the signers put it. They pledged to each other their "lives," "fortunes," and "sacred honor." Many lost their fortunes, some their lives, but despite their struggles, the signers stood firm for independence.

Step 3: Write About It Gather relevant information from print or digital sources and summarize or paraphrase what the Declaration of Independence is and how it marked the creation of a new nation (W 5.8).

Assessment
- ➢ Explain what the Declaration of Independence is and how it marked the creation of a new nation.

Extension Activities for "The Story of the Declaration of Independence"
- Work alone, or in pairs, to identify the 13 British colonies on a map.

- Make a list of ways you can show patriotism for our country? (Some possible answers include: Stand for the national anthem; Obey the laws; Vote; Hold elective office; Celebrate the Fourth of July and other national holidays such as Presidents Day, Memorial Day, and Veteran's Day; learn about the deeds of the Founders; visit historic sites)

Cut and Sort Vocabulary Cards

colonies	settlement
Great Britain	colonists
Parliament	representatives
patriot	taxes
Redcoats	intolerable
Minutemen	Continental Congress
Legislature	ignore
draft	declaration
independence	rights
parchment	pamphleteer

Vocabulary for "The Story of the Declaration of Independence"

colonies – lands or provinces that are far away from a country that rules over them

settlement – place where people make their permanent homes

Great Britain - island nation west of Europe made up originally of three older countries, England, Scotland, Wales and led by a King or Queen and Parliament

colonists – the people who live in the colonies

Parliament – the legislature of the British government

representatives – people who are chosen to speak for others from their community, colony or state

patriot – one who is loyal (or patriotic) to his or her country

taxes – money that governments collect from people or from the sale of goods to help pay the costs of government

Redcoats – British soldiers, who wore red uniforms

intolerable – describes something so bad that a person cannot live with it

Minutemen – armed civilians who pledged to be ready in a minute to defend their communities from attack

Continental Congress – gathering of representatives from the 13 colonies of British North America to decide colonial plans and policy

legislature – the part of a government that is made up of people elected to make rules and set taxes

ignore – pay no attention to

draft – to write an early version of something, or the version itself

declaration – announcement or full statement

independence – separateness, ability to stand on one's own

rights – the powers and opportunities a person or group should be able to get

parchment –a piece of animal skin treated to become a good, long-lasting surface for writing

pamphleteer – one who writes a pamphlet, or short booklet, on a single subject

The Story of the Declaration of Independence

There were thirteen **colonies** belonging to Britain that eventually became the United States. The first permanent **settlement**, Jamestown, became part of the colony of Virginia. The second settlement, Plymouth, became part of Massachusetts. In turn, Maryland, Rhode Island, Connecticut, North and South Carolina, New York, New Jersey, Delaware, Pennsylvania, and Georgia were either established by the British or taken over by them. The citizens of all 13 colonies considered themselves British citizens. Many came from Britain, but even those who came from other countries were British subjects.

British kings and queens and **Parliament** provided Americans with protection from attacks. They also provided some laws and appointed leaders, such as royal governors. Every British settlement on the Atlantic coast of North America was part of a colony.

In 1756, **Great Britain** went to war against France. One of the things that they were fighting about was control of North America. It was a very expensive war. After the British victory, Parliament decided that American **colonists** should pay new taxes to help pay for the war. After all, British soldiers had fought to protect Americans.

Many colonists did not like the **taxes**. They saw the taxes as a threat against their liberties as English citizens. Some complained that colonists did not get to elect **representatives** to Parliament, and so they should not be taxed by it. These people called themselves **patriots**, lovers of their country. When British troops, the **Redcoats**, stayed in American ports to help protect tax collectors, that angered patriots too.

In every one of the 13 colonies there were some patriots angry at English policies by 1775, but Massachusetts patriots showed the greatest concern. In 1770, a mob in Boston threatened some Redcoats who had fired their guns, killing 5 patriots. And late in 1773, some patriots dumped tea into the harbor to protest a new tea monopoly and a tax on tea. King George III and Parliament reacted by closing down Massachusetts' big port, Boston, and sending more troops. These *Intolerable Acts* (Coercive Acts) made patriots angry. They were afraid that the king would soon use troops against the colonists. To protect themselves, the patriots started collecting military supplies.

In April of 1775, English troops tried to capture two patriot leaders and military supplies outside Boston. Instead, they found bands of armed volunteers called **Minutemen** in Lexington and Concord. The Minutemen and Redcoats fired at each other, beginning the American Revolution. The Second **Continental Congress**, a gathering of representatives of all 13 colonies, began meeting a few weeks later in Philadelphia. The Congress made George Washington commander of the American forces. At the same time, it tried to convince King George to end the conflict peacefully.

King George **ignored** the colonists' complaints. He declared the colonies were in rebellion. By early January, 1777, British forces had attacked three other towns, from Portland, Maine (then known as Falmouth, Massachusetts) to Norfolk, Virginia. Many patriots, including the **pamphleteer** Thomas Paine, argued that the colonies should stop being part of Great Britain. Some members of Congress wanted to be sure that Americans in all the colonies wanted **independence**. Congress asked citizens to tell their representatives how they felt. Towns, counties, colonial **legislatures** and groups of citizens wrote them calling for independence.

In June, the Continental Congress created a committee of five members to **draft** a statement, or **declaration**, of independence. With the declaration being created, Congress would decide what to do. The declaration would need to say why the colonies were leaving the British Empire and announce their independence. Thomas Jefferson of Virginia was on the committee. The other four, including Benjamin Franklin of Pennsylvania, and John Adams of Massachusetts, decided Jefferson should write the first draft. They would all review it before giving it to the Congress.

Jefferson wrote his draft in a few days, using some wording from previous colonial declarations. He wanted to capture commonly held ideas about the basis of government. The phrase he wrote that became the most famous was "all men are created equal." The draft declared that King George had done many things that were unfair and harmful to the colonies. It said that the people of the colonies had a **right** to create a new national government for themselves, one that would not have a king at all.

On July 2, 1776 representatives of all of the 13 colonies voted to become independent of Great Britain and form the United States. They then spent two days working on the declaration. They revised it to make Jefferson's draft the best announcement of the new nation that they could make.

On July 4, the Continental Congress voted to use the edited version of the Declaration of Independence.

When the declaration was accepted, two officials signed it, the President of the Congress, John Hancock and Secretary Charles Thomson. Congress sent it immediately to a printer for copies to be sent throughout the colonies.

In many cities and towns the Declaration was read publicly. In some places the ringing of church bells celebrated the declaration. George Washington ordered it read to the troops so that they would know that a new nation depended upon them. A few weeks later, a special handwritten copy was created on parchment and signed by members of Congress.

Congress had decided that the United States should be independent on July 2, 1776. However, we celebrate July 4 because that is the day that the Declaration of Independence was first signed.

Many celebrations of the "nation's birthday" include readings of the Declaration of Independence. Americans think of the document most often as a statement of the country's ideas.

Today the **parchment** copy, signed by the representatives of the states in August 1776, is on display at the National Archives in Washington, D.C.

This lesson was adapted from The History Channel.

Fifth grade students deciding whether they should sign the *Declaration of Independence*.

Lesson 9: Thomas Paine's *The American Crisis* and the Brutal Winter at Valley Forge

Supporting Questions
- What was the impact of Thomas Paine's *The American Crisis*?
- What were the conditions at Valley Forge during the brutal winter of 1777-78?

Activity #1 Thomas Paine and *The American Crisis*

Materials needed: For each student, a copy of **Thomas Paine** (Handout # 9.1, page 52) and **Excerpts from *The American Crisis*** (Handout # 9.2, page 53).

Step 1: Reciprocal Reading Distribute a copy of **Thomas Paine** (Handout # 9.1). For easy reference, have students number each paragraph.

Students form pairs and read **Thomas Paine**, one paragraph at a time. After one student reads the first paragraph, his/her partner asks a question that comes to mind about the reading. The reader answers the question or, if needed, they both refer to the paragraph to identify the answer. Students than switch roles and read the next paragraph. Each set of partners always gets to ask questions as well as read a paragraph and answer questions.

This technique teaches students to focus intently on what they are reading by designing and asking questions (RI 5.2).

For the first time, it is recommended the teacher have a pair of students model the process of reciprocal reading. Plan enough time to be sure the students understand the process. Partners continue reading each paragraph and asking and answering questions.

At the end of the process, have one or two students summarize the reading (SL 5.2). In collaborative groups, have students discuss, "What was the impact of Thomas Paine's *American Crisis*?" (SL 5.1)

Step 2: *The American Crisis* Select a student to read aloud this excerpt from *The American Crisis*.

> **from *AMERICAN CRISIS* by Thomas Paine**
>
> **These are the times
> that try men's souls.**
>
> **The summer soldier
> and the sunshine patriot will,
> in this crisis,
> shrink from service
> of their country;**
>
> **but he that stands it now,
> deserves the love and thanks
> of man and woman.**

Discussion Questions: In pairs or small groups, students engage in a collaborative discussion of the following questions (SL 5.1).

- What is Paine referring to with "These are the times that try men's souls?"
- Have you ever faced any times that have tried your soul? (Covid-19?) How did you handle it?
- What does Paine mean by the phrase "summer solider and the sunshine patriot?"

Step 3: Excerpts from *The American Crisis* Distribute copies of Handout # 9.2. Introduce the word **tyranny** and discuss its meaning as cruel or harsh treatment by a government or ruler (RI 5.6).

Select 13 students who are powerful readers to read the selection. Encourage them to practice their lines with a partner who can give them suggestions, such as stand tall, speak slowly with conviction, face you audience and give them eye contact. When it is their turn, students stand at their desk to deliver their lines.

Have students respond to the following questions in a general class discussion.

- What is the point Thomas Paine is making in *The American Crisis*? To whom is he appealing?
- How would you have responded to Paine?
- According to Paine, what makes a true leader and patriot?

Activity #2 The Winter at Valley Forge

Materials needed: For each student, a copy of **Thomas Paine** (Handout #9.1 page 52) and *The American Crisis* (Handout #9.2, page 53). If available, a copy of *The Winter at Valley Forge* by James E. Knight and/or other print or digital sources.

Valley Forge Have students read accounts from multiple print and digital sources of the bitter winter at Valley Forge, 1777-78. The historical fiction book, *The Winter at Valley Forge - Survival and Victory* by James E. Knight, is recommended reading. Using a diary format, a soldier chronicles the harsh winter colonial soldiers spend at Valley Forge. The text and detailed illustrations evoke the personal suffering along with pertinent historical content. The descriptions are helpful for the writing activity at the end of this lesson.

Activity #3 Illustrations of an American Artist

American artists during the Revolution made sketches to illustrate the hardships soldiers faced during the winter at Valley Forge. The illustrations are done in pencil because it was so cold that ink or paint would freeze. Felix Darley, an early American book illustrator, sketched pictures of events during the American Revolution, including a series of sketches of the winter at Valley Forge. Encourage students to try doing a pencil sketch in the style of Darley.

For generations after the Revolution, artists painted pictures of Valley Forge to show the determination and heroism of American soldiers. Washington is often pictured with his troops at Valley Forge and some show Prussian Baron Friedrich Wilhelm von Steuben training American troops.

Art Analysis – Have students search for paintings or sketches that depict life at Valley Forge. As you view a work of art, ask students, "Based upon what you observe, list three things you might infer from this work of art? What questions does this work of art raise? Where could you find the answers? If you could speak with the artist, what is a question you would like to ask him/her?"

Activity #4 Write About Valley Forge

Step 1: Prewriting Conclude the lesson by having students assume the role of a soldier in winter quarters at Valley Forge. As a pre-writing activity, use the resources from this lesson to help students create a "word bank of academic language" to describe the severe winter conditions (RI 5.4). The "Word Bank" examples might include:

Nouns	Conditions at Valley Forge	
General George Washington	piercing wind	courage
Baron von Steuban	bleak and lonely	urgent need for shelter
Schuylkill River	men dressed in rags	daily rations and famine
General Howe	no uniforms	extreme cold and fatigue
Philadelphia	few have shoes	skirmish with the enemy
Quartermaster	buckskin shirts	typhus and smallpox
Continental soldiers	breeches	desertions and re-enlistments
Marquis de Lafayette	rifles and powder	daily drill, issue orders
Thomas Paine	muskets, bayonets	determination and heroism

Step 2: Prompt Write a letter or diary entries to chronicle your experiences and the conditions of the encampment at Valley Forge during the brutal winter of 1777-78 (W 5.3).

Directions: Write a letter or diary entries using descriptive details and clear event sequences.
- Orient the reader by establishing the conditions of the encampment at Valley Forge during the brutal winter of 1777-78.
- Use narrative techniques, such as dialogue and description to develop the experiences and events or to show your response to the situation.
- Use a variety of transitional words, phrases, or clauses to manage the sequence of events.
- Use sensory details to convey experiences and events precisely.
- Provide a conclusion that follows from the narrated experiences or events.

Assessment
➢ Write a letter or diary entries where you assume the role of a soldier in winter quarters at Valley Forge. Weave academic language into the letter or diary entries in an interesting way. Demonstrate an in-depth understanding of the severe winter conditions, support all mains ideas with facts. and provide substantial supported evidence.

Thomas Paine

Thomas Paine was a writer who was born and raised in England. He came to America in 1774 and soon became a strong advocate for the American cause.

He enlisted in the Continental Army and served as an aide to General Nathaniel Greene. In December 1776, within a year of the publication of his popular pamphlet *Common Sense*, he wrote a series of pamphlets entitled *The American Crisis* in which he described the problems confronting the new American nation.

Washington's forces had been defeated in the field and the prospects for winning the war with Britain seemed remote. The American troops were greatly outnumbered by the British. Many troops were ready to give up and reconcile with Great Britain.

Paine called upon men and women to serve their country in this time of need and not to back off when winning looked hopeless. Paine called for Americans to assume true leadership and patriotism in this time of crisis.

Paine wrote *The American Crisis* – reportedly using a battle drum for a desk – by the light of campfire to boost morale.

He left the camp for Philadelphia to have copies printed, which Washington ordered to be read aloud to his men on Christmas Eve 1776.

After it was read, the American troops crossed the Delaware and launched a surprise attack at Trenton. The American victory infused new life in the patriot's cause.

     Excerpts from *The American Crisis*

Select 13 students to stand and read, with strength and passion, the following sentences.

1. These are the times that try men's souls.

2. The summer soldier and the sunshine patriot will, in this crisis, shrink from the service of his country; but he that stands it NOW, deserves the love and thanks of man and woman.

3. Tyranny, like hell, is not easily conquered; yet we have this consolation with us, that the harder the conflict the more glorious the triumph.

4. What we obtain too cheap, we esteem too lightly; 'tis dearness only that gives very thing its value.

5. Heaven knows how to put a proper price upon its goods; and it would be strange indeed, if so celestial an article as FREEDOM should not be highly rated.

6. Britain, with an army to enforce her tyranny, has declared that she has a right (*not only to* TAX) but "to BIND us in ALL CASES WHATSOEVER," and if being *bound in that manner*, is not slavery, than is there no such a thing as slavery upon earth . . . .

7. I call not upon a few, but upon all: not on *this* state or *that* state, but on *every* state; up and help us; lay your shoulders to the wheel; better have too much force than too little, when so great an object is at stake.

8. Let it be told to the future world, that in the depth of winter, when nothing but hope and virtue could survive, that the city and the country, alarmed at one common danger, came forth to meet and to repulse it.

9. Say not that thousands are gone, turn out your tens of thousands; throw not the burden of the day upon Providence, but *"show your faith by your works,"* that God may bless you.

10. It matters not where you live, or what rank of life you hold, the evil or the blessing will reach you all. . .

11. The heart that feels not now, is dead: the blood of his children will curse his cowardice, who shrinks back at a time when a little might have saved the whole and make them happy.

12. I love the man that can smile in trouble, that can gather strength from distress, and grow brace by reflection.

13. 'Tis the business of little minds to shrink; but he whose heart is firm, and whose conscience approves his conduct, will pursue his principles unto death. . .

Lesson 10: The Articles of Confederation

Supporting Questions
- What was the purpose of the Articles of Confederation?
- What were the weaknesses of the Articles of Confederation?

Activity # 1 What Do We Do About A Government?
Explain to the students that during the war, the colonies worked together because they were fighting for a common cause. After the war was won, the 13 states set up governments that were different from each other. Most people thought of themselves as a citizen of their state rather than of one country. The people referred to themselves as "New Yorkers" rather than "Americans." Once they were independent, the job was to turn 13 former British colonies into one single country.
- What do you think the colonists will do to create a new government?
- What problems do you think the colonial leaders might face?

The idea of people making their own laws was brand new. At that time, most countries were ruled by kings. The new American citizens did not want a powerful national government. They were afraid of a strong Congress and a strong President.
- Why do you think the former colonists were afraid of a strong national government with a strong Congress and a strong President? (They feared a large, all-powerful government ruling their lives. They had just fought a war of independence to get rid of a strong national government.)
- What could be the problem with a strong national government?
- What could be the problem with a weak national government?
- What type of government do you think they will want to create?

Activity # 2 Articles of Confederation
Explain to the students that the Articles of Confederation were written during the war and finally ratified when Maryland agreed in 1781 after the western land question was settled. Written mostly by the Delaware delegate, John Dickinson, they outlined rules for a "firm league of friendship." They loosely united the states into a confederation, but each state still acted like a separate country. Dickinson preferred strong states and a weak national government. He wanted a *confederation*, a government made up of a group of partners who keep all the power to themselves. There would be no higher power. The central government would serve mainly as an advisor.

Step 1: Research the Articles of Confederation Using multiple print and digital sources, read information about who wrote the Articles of Confederation, what was its purpose, and identify its weaknesses (RI 5.6). John Dickinson wrote most of the first draft of the Articles of Confederation. It did not give the Congress much power to do anything. The only President was the President of the Congress, and he had no power. Congress could declare war, but it could not raise an army without the state's permission. It could pass laws for the nation, but it had no way of enforcing the laws. The biggest problem was money. Each state made its own money and had its own way of taxing.
- What problems were caused by the weaknesses of the United States government under the Articles of Confederation?
- How much power is enough power? How much power can you give up and still be able to keep your freedom?

Step 2: Consensus Divide students into small groups. Ask the class, "If you had an extra ten minutes of recess today, what one activity would your group do?" (SL 5.1)

Most groups will decide fairly quickly on a specific activity. Once the groups are in agreement, let each group announce its choice to the class.

Explain that now the **entire** class must decide upon one activity that **everyone** will participate in if given ten minutes extra recess. Observe students as they try to get organized and reach a consensus (SL 5.1).

When the decision has been made, if in fact they are able to reach a consensus, ask them questions such as:
- What problems were you faced with in trying to reach an agreement?
- Why do you think that as a small group you could function toward a goal, but once you had to decide as an entire class, you found it more difficult?

Lack of consensus was the reason the Articles of Confederation failed. With states printing their own money (valid only within their borders), taxing out-of-state goods, and failing to contribute to the national treasury funds necessary for the federal government to operate, the failure to cooperate almost caused the new country to fail.

Step 3: Equal Votes The Articles of Confederation limited the authority of Congress by requiring 9 of 13 states to agree before a law was passed. However, the states seldom agreed on anything. Each wanted its own way. Each state had an equal vote even though some states were small and others were large. For example, even though Rhode Island had 68,000 people and Virginia had 747,000 people, they each had only one vote.

To illustrate the problem of the states equal votes, divide your class into 13 groups so that some of the groups have only 1 student and other groups have 2, 3, 4 or 5 students. (For example, a class of 32 might have groups of 5, 4, 4, 3, 3, 3, 2, 2, 2, 1, 1, 1, and 1.) Present the students with a decision to make such as **creating a set of class rules**. Give each group one vote. 9 out of 13 of the groups must agree on a rule before it can be accepted. (Note: All 13 states were needed to change the Articles.)

- Were you able to agree on a set of class rules? Why or why not? What challenges did you have to overcome?
- Just as it was difficult to agree on class rules, what are the things the newly independent states could not agree on?

Step 4: What Happened Next? Explain to the students that it took six years to develop a workable form of government. On May 25, 1787, 55 delegates, from all states except Rhode Island, arrived in Philadelphia for the Constitutional Convention. James Madison got the convention organized. The delegates were supposed to revise the Articles of Confederation, but Madison thought rewriting it was a bad idea. He knew he would have to convince a lot of the delegates of that, so he read all he could about governments all over the world and throughout history. He took the best ideas he could find and wrote them in notebooks and brought them to the convention.

They agreed to have Virginia's governor, Edmund Randolph, present the plan to the Constitutional Convention. It was called the Virginia Plan. It made the work much easier for the delegates because they had a document that served as a starting point.

Lesson 11: The Treaty (Peace) of Paris

Supporting Questions

- How did the British army compare with the Continental army?
- What were the reasons for the victory over the British at Yorktown?

Activity #1 Compare the Armies

Step 1: The Continental Army versus the British Army The British army clearly had many advantages over the Continental army. Using multiple print and digital sources, complete the chart below comparing the British army with the Continental army (sample answers included).

After completing the chart, have students role-play a conversation in which they tell a partner why he or she should join the Continental Army. Support your explanation with reasons and evidence (SL 5.3).

	Continental Army	**British Army**
Geography	Were fighting on their own land and for their own homes and for their freedom	Were fighting for the King on a foreign land 3000 miles away from home
Number of soldiers	Generally, had no more than 10,000 soldiers at any one time, many went home at harvest time or left when they did not get paid	Large army with about 50,000 soldiers
Experience and supplies	Had never fought together as an army, many had no uniforms, and they used whatever weapons they had on hand	Made up of professional soldiers with the best training, the most experienced officers, and the newest weapons
Fighting strategy	Fought in irregular lines and from hiding places	Fought side by side in straight lines
Assistance	Received help from several other countries and from some Native Americans	Mercenaries, or hired soldiers, and some Native American allies
Commanders	George Washington	Thomas Gage, Charles Cornwallis

Step 2: The Battle at Yorktown Read to students the following information:

General Washington's plan was to keep his army moving, hopefully tiring out the British forces. He lost several battles in New York and New Jersey. In October 1777, the Americans had won a major battle at Saratoga, New York. Their luck was changing. When the French heard of this spectacular victory, they decided to support the Americans. They declared war on England on July 10, 1778. Soon, boats filled with supplies and French soldiers were arriving in the colonies.

The British General Cornwallis decided to strike the southern colonies. From 1779 to 1780, Cornwallis marched his soldiers through South and North Carolina. He won victories at Savannah and Camden. In 1781, he ordered his army north to Virginia. By August, seven thousand British were camped in the small town of Yorktown, Virginia.

Washington, and a French general named Rochambeau, sent their armies numbering more than sixteen thousand men on a 500-mile journey from Rhode Island to Yorktown, Virginia. Cornwallis did not worry. He thought that he could always load his men onto ships and escape.

Once at Yorktown, the American and French armies worked through the night to dig deep trenches. The British found the next morning, September 30, 1781, that they were surrounded. French warships blocked the York River, preventing British ships from bringing more troops to Yorktown and preventing their escape.

The Battle at Yorktown lasted 14 days. About 600 British soldiers and 100 American soldiers died fighting. The Americans had heavy guns and more cannons than the British. On October 19th, Britain surrendered to America. The war was over at last.

In a period of eight years of bloody war, a colonial army with no experience defeated one of the most powerful armies in the world to become a new nation – The United States of America.

A group of fifth graders ask, "*Why on Earth would we want to take on the most powerful army in the world*?"

Step 3: Write About It Have students do a short research project using multiple print and digital sources to find out how the French helped the Americans win the Battle of Yorktown.

Using the information from several sources and information from the chart in Step 1, write a paragraph to analyze why the Continental army was able to defeat the British army at Yorktown (W 5.7).

Activity #2 The Peace (Treaty) of Paris

Step 1: Resolving Conflicts Explain to students that the Battle of Yorktown did not end the Revolutionary War. The Treaty (Peace) of Paris did that.

To help students understand how people resolve conflicts, have them work in collaborative groups to respond to the following questions (SL 5.1):

- What types of arguments or fights do people sometimes have with each other? What types of actions do they take when they have an argument or a fight? What are the consequences of these actions? How do they "negotiate" or talk with one another to work out an agreement? Is everyone always happy with the agreement? Why or why not? What types of arguments or fights do countries sometimes have with each other?
- What types of actions do they take when they have an argument or a fight? What are the consequences of these actions?
- How do countries "negotiate" or talk with one another to work out an agreement? Is everyone always happy with the agreement? Why or why not?

- What was the argument, or fight, that the British and the Colonists had with each other? What types of actions did the British take? What were the consequences? What types of actions did the Colonists take? What were the consequences?

Explain to the students that to "negotiate" an end to the Revolutionary War, the British and the Americans signed a treaty in 1783. A **treaty** is an agreement between countries (RI 5.4). Two years passed between the British surrender at Yorktown and the signing of an official peace treaty in Paris.

The terms of the treaty between the British and the Americans, signed on September 3, 1783, formally recognized the United States as an independent nation. The British monarch and Parliament had to accept American independence and remove British soldiers from American soil.

It also established the boundaries of the new nation at an imaginary line through the Great Lakes in the North, the Mississippi River in the West, and the 31st parallel (at Florida) in the South. **For a helpful map of the treaty boundaries, go to** https://www.nationalgeographic.org/photo/treaty-1783/

In addition, Americans were guaranteed fishing rights in the waters off British Newfoundland and Nova Scotia.

A further clause called for the American government to treat the Tories or Loyalists fairly and to compensate them for any loss of property incurred during the fighting.

Step 2: Write About It Write a paragraph to explain at least two effects of the Treaty of Paris in 1783 between the British and the Americans (W 5.7).

Step 3: Classroom Treaty Ask students what type of conflict arises in the classroom or on the playground? Discuss the conflict and negotiate an agreement or "treaty" that can end the conflict. For example, students may have disagreements over who gets to use the sports equipment at recess time. In a negotiated treaty, students may agreement upon a procedure to determine who gets to use the equipment each day. Post the "treaty" and give it a name such as "The Treaty of Sports Equipment – October 2020."

Step 4: Discussion Questions

- Suppose the Patriots had lost the Revolutionary War and Great Britain had maintained control of the colonies. Would the United States ever have become a country? Why or why not?
- What would have happened to the patriots such as Thomas Jefferson, John Adams and Benjamin Franklin?

Assessment

- ➢ Role-play a conversation in which you tell a partner why he or she should join the Continental Army. Support your explanation with reasons and evidence.
- ➢ Write a paragraph to analyze why the Continental army was able to defeat the British army at Yorktown
- ➢ Write a paragraph to explain at least two effects of the Treaty of Paris in 1783 between the British and the Americans?

Lesson 12: Freedom's Journey

Supporting Question: What were the key events of the American Revolution?

<table>
<tr><td>

<u>Materials needed</u>: For each student, a copy of **Sequencing Events of the American Revolution** (Handout #12.1, page 61); for each **pair** of students, a copy of **Organizing the Events of the American Revolution** (Handout #12.2, pages 62-63)

</td></tr>
</table>

Activity # 1 Sequencing Events of the American Revolution

Provide students with a copy of **Sequencing Events of the American Revolution** (Handout #12.1). Instruct students to use the timeline developed in Lesson 1 to place the following events in their proper sequence by numbering them from 1 to 8, with 1 being the earliest event and 8 being the latest event.

Order	Event	Proper Sequence
______	Treaty of Paris	8
______	Boston Tea Party	3
______	Stamp Act	1
______	Signing of the Declaration of Independence	4
______	Boston Massacre	2
______	Articles of Confederation are ratified by the states	6
______	Continental army spends the winter at Valley Forge	5
______	American victory at the Battle of Yorktown	7

Activity # 2 Organizing the Events of the American Revolution

Provide students with a copy of the following chart **Organizing the Events of the American Revolution** (Handout #12.2.) Using multiple print and digital sources, have students work together, in pairs, to complete the chart (RL 5.5, RL 5.6, W 5.8).

Date	Event	Key People	Challenges Colonists Faced (CAUSE)	Responses to the Challenges (EFFECT)
1765	Stamp Act	Patriots, Sons of Liberty, King George III		protests
1770			Having British soldiers in their city (Boston)	Used as propaganda to gather support for independence
1773			Taxes imposed by the British Parliament (The Tea Act)	Angered British leaders; Parliament passed the Coercive Acts (Intolerable Acts)
1776		Thomas Jefferson, John Adams, Benjamin Franklin	Colonists began to think they could rule themselves; Thomas Paine called for Independence	

1778	Troops trained at Valley Forge			Other nations helped the Patriot cause; troops became more organized
1781	Articles of Confeder-ation	John Dickinson		
1781			Defeat British army	
1783	Treaty of Paris		Fighting dragged on for more than two years; Negotiate a peace treaty	

Activity #3 What do you think? Discuss the following questions:

- If you lived during the time of the Revolutionary War, would you more likely be a Patriot or a Loyalist?
- Had you lived during the time of the War, what Revolutionary War leader would you have admired most?
- Do you think the Revolutionary War could have been avoided? Why or why not?

Activity #4 Catchy Headlines – From Different Points of View

With the students, review several newspapers focusing on the headlines. Discuss the style of writing used – short, not a complete sentence, eye-catching, snappy, etc.

From the viewpoint of a rebel, a loyalist, a British citizen who supports King George or another person, select one of the events from the timeline (Handout #12.1) and write a "catchy" headline for the event as it might appear in the newspaper.

Assessment

- ➢ Place key events of the American Revolution in chronological order.
- ➢ Use multiple print and digital sources to identify events, key people, and the causes and effects of the American Revolution.
- ➢ Write a catchy headline for an event in the unit as written from the viewpoint of a rebel, a loyalist, a British citizen who supports King George, or another person.

Extended Activities

Writing News Stories To highlight some of the key events of the American Revolution, divide the class into 5 groups. Each group selects one of the key events featured in this unit.

Each newspaper should have articles including:

- a descriptive news story about the event, including who, what, when, where, why.
- an interview of a person involved with an event and write a news story using quotations.
- an advice column suggesting a solution to a problem related to the event.
- an editorial of a letter to the editor about the event.
- another type of article, of your choice.

Assemble the news articles for each event. Let each group determine the name of their newspaper, the date of the issue, and a design for masthead of the paper.

Handout #12.1

Sequencing Events of the American Revolution

Place the following events in their proper sequence by numbering them from 1 to 8, with 1 being the earliest event and 8 being the latest event.

Note: First, locate the date of each event and record it on the line to the <u>left</u> of the event. After recording all the dates, sequence the events. For reference, you may use the use the timeline in Handout #1.2 (page 13).

DATE   SEQUENCE

_____Treaty of Paris   _______

_____Boston Tea Party   _______

_____Stamp Act   _______

_____Signing of the Declaration of Independence   _______

_____Boston Massacre   _______

_____Articles of Confederation are ratified by the states _______

_____Continental army spends winter at Valley Forge   _______

_____American victory at the Battle of Yorktown   _______

Name_________________________________ Date___________________

Organizing the Events of the American Revolution

Working in pairs, complete the following chart using multiple print and digital sources.

Date	Event	Key People	Challenges Colonists Faced (CAUSE)	Responses to the Challenges (EFFECT)
1765	Stamp Act	Patriots, Sons of Liberty, King George III		protests
1770			Having British soldiers in their city (Boston)	Used as propaganda to gather support for independence
1773			Taxes imposed by the British Parliament (The Tea Act)	Angered British leaders; Parliament passed the Coercive Acts (Intolerable Acts)
1776		Thomas Jefferson, John Adams, Benjamin Franklin	Colonists began to think they could rule themselves; Thomas Paine called for Independence	
1778	Troops trained at Valley Forge			Other nations helped the Patriot cause; troops became more organized
1781	Articles of Confederation	John Dickinson		
1781			Defeat British army	
1783	Treaty of Paris ends the American Revolution		Fighting dragged on for more than two years; negotiate a peace treaty	

Name_______________________________________   Date_____________________

ANSWER KEY Organizing the Events of the American Revolution

(Answers may vary)

Date	Event	Key People	Challenges Colonists Faced (CAUSE)	Responses to the Challenges (EFFECT)
1765	Stamp Act	Patriots, Sons of Liberty, King George III	Parliament needed money to pay off the costs of the French and Indian War	Protests were quick and angry; delegates from nine colonies met as the Stamp Act Congress; No taxation without representation
1770	Boston Massacre	British soldiers; large crowd of angry colonists (Crispus Attucks)	Having British soldiers in their city (Boston)	Used as propaganda to gather support for independence
1773	Boston Tea Party	Sons of Liberty Dressed as Mohawk Indians	Taxes imposed by the British Parliament (The Tea Act)	Angered British leaders; Parliament passed the Coercive Acts (Intolerable Acts)
1776	Declaration of Independence	Thomas Jefferson, John Adams, Benjamin Franklin	Colonists began to think they could rule themselves; Thomas Paine called for independence	Formed a committee to write the Articles of Confederation; Colonial leaders united against Britain; the Revolutionary War
1778	Troops trained At Valley Forge	Von Steuben Washington American troops	Americans spent the Winter in cold and harsh conditions; Von Steuben trained the troops	Other nations helped the Patriot cause; troops became more organized
1781	Articles of Confederation	John Dickinson	A new government had to be formed	It brought the 13 independent states together and set up a national legislature
1781	British surrender to Americans at Yorktown	French military and naval forces Washington Cornwallis	Defeat British army	Treaty of Paris
1783	Treaty of Paris ends the American Revolution	Benjamin Franklin, John Adams, John Jay	Fighting dragged on for more than two years; Negotiate a peace treaty	Britain had to accept American independence and remove all British soldiers

Resources for The American Revolution

Adler, David. *The Picture Book of Benjamin Franklin*. Illustrated by John Wallner and Alexandra Wallner. Holiday House; Reprint edition, 2018. This easy-read biography surveys the life of Benjamin Franklin, highlighting his work as an inventor and statesman. Additional books in the David Adler easy-read biography series include: *The Picture Book of Paul Revere*, Reprint edition, 1997; *The Picture Book of Thomas Jefferson*. Reprint edition, 2018; *The Picture Book of George Washington*. Reprint edition, 2018.

Baretta, Gene. *Now & Ben: The Modern Inventions of Benjamin Franklin*. Square Fish, 2008. Explore the inventions of Benjamin Franklin and how they have stood the test of time.

Berleth, Richard. *Samuel's Choice*. Albert Whitman & Company. Reprint, 2012). The year is 1777 in this historical fiction book. A young slave must decide whether to defy his master and help the colonists by offering his boating skills to the Revolutionary soldiers.

Brady, Esther Wood. *Toliver's Secret*. Yearling; Reprint edition, 1993. When it becomes dangerous for her grandfather to smuggle secrets to General George Washington, a young girl takes over in this historical fiction book. Disguised as a boy, she crosses British lines to deliver her message.

Collier, James Lincoln and Christopher, *My Brother Sam is Dead*. Scholastic Paperbacks; unknown edition, 2005. This Newbery Honor book tells the story of Tim Meeker and the choice he must make as his family is being torn apart by the American Revolution. On the one hand, his brother Sam is a part of the Revolutionary army and he talks about defeating the British and becoming independent and free. But, most people in his town, including his father, are loyal supporters of the English king. Usually read by middle school students, avid fifth grade readers will enjoy the drama. Some teachers feel the book is to violent.

Davis, Burke. *Black Heroes of the American Revolution*. Odyssey Books Paperback, 1992. This book provides an account of the black soldiers, sailors, spies, scouts, guides, and wagoners who participated and sacrificed in the struggle for American independence.

Edwards, Pamela Duncan. *Boston Tea Party*. Illustrated by Henry Cole. Puffin Books; Reprint edition, 2016. Few of the many books on this topic are as captivating as this version of the famous "tea party" told in part by the English and colonial mice characters who were "eyewitnesses" to the events. Young children will enjoy the illustrations while adults appreciate the amount of content covered so effortlessly.

Forbes, Esther. *America's Paul Revere*. Pictures by Lynd Ward. HMH Books for Young Readers, 1990. This well-researched book narrates the varied life of Paul Revere, including his many trades and his civic involvement in early America. The reading is a little more challenging for fifth graders.

Freedman, Russell. *Give Me Liberty! The Story of the Declaration of Independence*. Holiday House; Reprint edition, 2002. Describes the events leading up to the Declaration of Independence as well as the personalities and politics behind its framing. Many primary source paintings are included. Good for student reading or teacher reference.

Fritz, Jean. *And Then What Happened, Paul Revere?* Pictures by Margot Tomes. Puffin Books; Reissue edition, 1996. This entertaining presentation portrays the era well and shows many facets of Colonial life and the events at Concord and Lexington. Additional books by Jean Fritz include: *Why Don't You Get a Horse, Sam Adams?* Illustrations by Trina Schart Hyman. Scott Foresman; Reissue edition, 2000; and, *Will You Sign Here, John Hancock.* Illustrations by Trina Schart Hyman. Puffin Books; Reprint edition, 1997.

Giblin, James Cross. *The Amazing Life of Benjamin Franklin.* Illustrated by Michael Dooling. Scholastic Press, 2006. This beautifully illustrated biography captures the varied life of the printer, inventor, and statesman who played an influential part in America's early history.

Gregory, Kristiana. *Winter of Red Snow: The Revolutionary War Diary of Abigail Jane Stewart.* Scholastic Inc.; Library Binding edition, 1996). This historical fiction story in the Dear America series presents a diary-like account by eleven-ear-old Abigail of life in Valley Forge from December 1777 to July 1778. She describes the action as General George Washington prepares his troops to fight the British.

Hakim, Joy. *From Colonies to Country 1735-1791.* New York: Oxford University Press, 3rd revised edition, 2007. Part of the series, "History of Us," this book covers American history from the French and Indian War to the Constitutional Convention. Hakim's writing style is designed to make history engaging for children.

Isaacs, Sally Senzell. *America in the Time of George Washington 1747-1803.* Heinemann, 1998. This book uses the life of George Washington as a reference to examine the history of the United States during the French and Indian War, the Revolutionary War, the time of the Continental Congress, and early years of the new nation.

January, Brendan. *The True Book of the Revolutionary War.* Children's Press, 2001. This large print book for young readers describes the events preceding, during, and following the American Revolution, from the Stamp Act in 1765 to the signing of the Treaty of Paris.

Knight, James E. *The Winter at Valley Forge – Survival and Victory.* Troll Communications, 1982. A soldier chronicles the harsh winter colonial soldiers, led by General George Washington, spend at Valley Forge during the winter of 1777-78. Although the book is historical fiction, the diary entries provide content information useful to help students understand the hardships endured.

Kroll, Steven. *The Boston Tea Party.* Illustrated by Peter Fiore. Holiday House, 1998. Beautiful illustrations enhance the story of the events preceding, during, and following the event which helped precipitate the American Revolution.

Lawson, Robert. *Mr. Revere and I: Being an Account of certain Episodes in the Career of Paul Revere, Esq. as Revealed by his Horse.* Little, Brown Books for Young Readers; Reprint edition,1988. This entertaining book tells the life of the Revere family, and the doings of the Sons of Liberty from the point of view of Scheherazade, Paul Revere's horse.

Levy, Elizabeth. *If You Were There When They Signed the Constitution.* Illustrations by Joan Holub. Scholastic Paperbacks; Updated edition, 1992. This question and answer book takes you behind the locked doors of Philadelphia's State House during the summer of 1787.

Longfellow, Henry Wadsworth. *Paul Revere's Ride*. Illustrated by Ted Rand. Puffin, 1996. This is a beautifully illustrated version of the immortal poem about Paul Revere and his famous midnight ride.

McGovern, Ann. *The Secret Soldier*. The Story of Deborah Sampson. Scholastic Paperbacks, 1990. This is the historical fiction story of a young girl who disguises herself as a boy to fight in the American Revolution.

Moore, Kay. *If You Lived at the Time of the American Revolution*. Illustrated by Daniel O'Leary. Scholastic Paperbacks, 1998. Have you ever wondered what it would be like to live during the American Revolution? This informative book answers many questions about the day-to-day life in the colonies from the viewpoint of both the patriots and the loyalists.

Murphy, Jim. *A Young Patriot: The American Revolution as Experienced by One Boy*. Clarion Books, 1998. Murphy tells the story of the American Revolution through the eyes of Joseph Plumb Martin who enlisted in the army in 1776, at the age of 15.

O'Dell, Scott. *Sarah Bishop*. Houghton Mifflin School, 1992. Told in the first person, this historical fiction novel is a gripping story of the pain and suffering caused by the Revolution. Left alone after the deaths of her father and brother, who take opposites in the War for Independence, Sarah Bishop flees from the British who seek to arrest her.

Osborne, Mary Pope. *Revolutionary War on Wednesday*. Random House Books for Young Readers, 2000. If it is Wednesday, it must be Revolutionary War day with Jack and Annie, stars of the Magic Tree House series. General George Washington is about to lead his army in a sneak attack against their enemy. But terrible weather is making him question his plans. Can Jack and Annie keep history on track? The fate of the country rests in their hands!

Schanzer, Rosalyn. *George vs. George: The American Revolution as Seen from Both Sides*. National Geographic Children's Books; Reprint edition, 2007. This narrative shows history from different points of view, that of George Washington and King George. The illustrations and the engaging quote bubbles bring the Revolution to life.

Trusiani, Lisa *The Story of George Washington: A Biography Book for New Readers* (The Story Of: A Biography Series for New Readers). Rockridge Press, 2020. This is a fun, colorful book about the life of George Washington, fighting for independence and building a country.

Turner, Ann. *Katie's Trunk*. Illustrations by Ron Himler. Aladdin; Reprint edition, 1997. Based on a true incident that happened to one of the author's ancestors, this book tells the story of Katie, whose family is not sympathetic to rebel soldiers during the American Revolution, hides under clothes in her mother's wedding trunk when they invade her home.

Weidt, Maryann N. *Revolutionary Poet: A Story About Phillis Wheatley*. Lerner Classroom.1997. This biography traces the life and accomplishments of Phillis Wheatley from her arrival in America on a slave ship in 1761, learning to write in the Wheatley home, her trip to England, and the hard years of selling her books during the Revolution.